"Bill Newman is… a compassionate human being. He cares deeply about the rights and freedoms of all of us, and by the time you finish reading *When The War Came Home*, you will, too. This is an intimate, generous, thought-provoking collection written with wit, candor, and heart."

— *Lesléa Newman, author of* October Mourning:
A Song For Matthew Shepard

"Deeply moving, extremely insightful, surprisingly provocative, and often funny, *When The War Came Home* is engaging and inspiring. I hope this book is volume one of a series!"

— *Rev. Andrea Avazian*

"Bill Newman… gives us a lens to see how the powers that be need to be transformed today can be transformed. To read this book is to know why we, in the words of Hebrew scripture, 'need his voice for just such a time as this.'"

— *Rev. Peter Ives, the reverend of the*
"Reverend and the Rabbi" segment on the Bill Newman Radio Show

"A history of the peace and justice movement… told with humor and heart, social justice and sex, weeping and weed."

— *Monte Belmonte, radio host on 93.9/The River*
and co-host of the Bill Newman Radio Show

"This book is a welcome reminder that America's cultural revolution was about more than sex, drugs, and music. It was about justice and equality and a healthy skepticism of authority. Bill Newman does his generation proud."

– *Attorney Richard Evans, drug reform advocate,*
former Board Member, NORML

"It helps to remember… that soldiers waged war at Kent State, that some of us were alive at the birth of rock 'n' roll, that other births are at the core of who we are. *When the War Came Home* serves us well."

— *Jon Weissman, Coordinator, Western Mass. Jobs with Justice*

Bill Newman is a born writer—observant, imaginative, and obsessive about getting life down on paper before the moment and the meaning dissipate. This book, by turns wise and funny, heartfelt and searing, written in a voice that demands, deserves, and rewards our close attention, will make you gasp and weep and laugh.

— *Barry Werth, author of* The Antidote: Inside The World
of New Pharma *and* The Scarlet Professor

WHEN THE WAR CAME HOME

Bill Newman

Bill Newman

Levellers Press

AMHERST, MASSACHUSETTS

All rights reserved including the right of
reproduction in whole or in part in any form.

Cover image used with permission: May 4 Collection,
Kent State University Libraries, Special Collections and Archives.

Some pieces here have appeared in an earlier from in *The Massachusetts Review,*
the *Daily Hampshire Gazette,* and *Hampshire Life* magazine.
Permissions gratefully acknowledged.

Thanks to poet Greg Orr for permission to use "Making Beasts."

Published by *Levellers Press,* Amherst, Massachusetts

Printed in the United States of America

ISBN 978-1-937146-43-6

For Dale

Contents

WHEN THE WAR CAME HOME

WHAT LASTS?

It was 1968, and I hated seeing people locked up in cages. I still do.

I was eighteen then and working in the New York City criminal courts for a new criminal justice reform organization, the Vera Institute of Justice. It was my first job on Antioch College's work-study program.

We Antioch students would sit at a beat-up metal desk behind Lupe, the arraignment session clerk, a man about fifty we guessed, who had a big laugh, a welcoming smile, and a terrible toupee that in the front rested a full one-quarter inch above his head. Every day we tried to not look at the chasm between Lupe's head and his hair although, honestly, sometimes it was hard not to.

Our job as "screeners" was to review the criminal charges, record, and police reports of every person arrested in Manhattan to determine who might qualify for Vera's experimental diversion and rehabilitation program, The Manhattan Court Employment Project (MCEP). Most defendants were quickly disqualified because of their previous convictions, because they had been brought in on drug charges, or because they were facing serious felonies. Or they were women. At that time the program only accepted men.

If a defendant made the initial cut, we'd fasten his paperwork to a clipboard, leave our cocoon behind Lupe to exit the clerk's office into the courtroom, and then navigate our way through prosecutors, police and probation officers, defendants, and guards, to the thick, heavy door that opened into the holding pens. Those pens—those jail cells—were coated with grime and smelled like piss, and a stray hypodermic needle often lay on the concrete floor under one of the metal benches bolted to the wall. The too-few benches for too many men meant that many would stand for three, four, five, or six hours waiting their turn to be herded into court for arraignment. Many of our prospective clients, as we interviewed them through the cell's iron bars, would grab them tight with both hands and squeeze them in a ferocious grip, almost as if they thought they could shake them loose.

Those men, mostly young, all poor, and overwhelmingly black and Hispanic, had entered a maze from which few escape—the criminal justice system. But Vera's Manhattan Court Employment Project offered a map that showed a way out. When a judge assigned a defendant to the program, his pending criminal charges would be held in abeyance while he participated in the required counseling (the counselors were all ex-cons who had served an average of eight years in upstate prisons for serious felonies), succeeded at holding a job or completing a job-training program, and stayed out of trouble. If he did all that, there would be no trial, no plea; rather, the charges would be dropped. Unfortunately, in our interviews we'd often become privy to drug use or mental health problems or outstanding warrants that hadn't yet caught up with the defendant—facts that would disqualify him. But sometimes all the information would check out, no bad facts would emerge, and then we screeners would celebrate.

Our task then became—either that day or at the next court appearance—to convince an assistant district attorney to reduce the felony charges to misdemeanors so that the defendant could enter the project. If we succeeded at that, we next would consult with the public defender about arguments to proffer to the judge. (Men wearing black robes—they were all men then—had the final word on whether a man facing charges could enter Vera's program.) The defense lawyers often would ask us to make the presentation, to explain, if asked, why offering a job and a future to young men accused of crimes did not amount to rewarding the law-breakers.

At its core, our argument was straightforward. Vera's program offered hope in a system where hopelessness constituted the common denominator. That sliver of optimism almost always convinced even the most recalcitrant judge to grant our motion and assign the defendant to the Court Employment Project. For eighteen- and nineteen-year-old college students, this was pretty heady stuff.

For us, the first group of Antioch students to work at Vera, the job was supposed to last one quarter—three months—but we stayed for nine. The college eventually informed us that, unless we returned to campus in Yellow Springs, Ohio, for a study quarter, we'd lose our status as matriculating students. That ultimatum mattered. If Antioch couldn't certify me as a full-time student, I'd lose the draft deferment that was allowing me to escape the war in Vietnam.

So I returned to school. But I couldn't leave behind what I had seen and heard in those courtrooms and holding pens. Images and words had been seared into my consciousness, and I would apply to law school and become a criminal defense and civil rights lawyer, and later an attorney with the American Civil Liberties Union, in no small measure because of what I heard, saw, and felt there.

At that time, you were breaking a federal law if you didn't have your draft card *"in your personal possession at all times."* It said so right on the card.

Of course, many of us broke that law, and why not? Who would know whether you were carrying your draft card?

My overly cautious or unduly paranoid mind supplied an answer. Some cop might bust me for disorderly conduct at a demonstration or stop me for speeding, and then turn me over to the feds for breaking the Selective Service law. So I often carried my draft card in my wallet.

In contrast, some principled anti-Vietnam War activists publicly broke draft laws. They either refused to register with the Selective Service System or, having registered, later burned their draft cards or mailed them back to the government. When ordered to report, they refused induction and ended up being sent to federal prison.

Randy Kehler, who two decades later I'd help represent in his war-tax-resistance cases, took that path. Sentenced to two years, Randy served twenty-two months, six at the Safford, Arizona, federal prison, and sixteen more at the one in La Tuna, Texas. Daniel Ellsberg attributes his decision to publicly release the top secret study called *The Pentagon Papers* to meeting Randy and hearing him speak about his impending imprisonment and the reasons he willingly was going to jail.

But most college students did not emulate Randy and his principled, line-in-the-sand, I-will-not-cooperate-with-the-machinery-of-war stance. Rather, we accepted our draft deferments, which kept the war, the army, and the accompanying question—how to permanently evade military service—a safe distance from our daily and sometimes solipsistic lives.

Of necessity, we lived with the uneasiness of knowing the day would come when the deferment would expire. Then we would need to either pursue conscientious objector status; or devise a medical or psychological malady to force the army to reject us; or hire a draft lawyer to finagle some legalistic way out; and, if none of these worked, to accept being imprisoned or to flee to Canada.

We did not, at least I did not, worry incessantly. To an eighteen-year-old, three or four years in the future can feel far away indeed, so the inevitable expiration of my deferment felt like a chronic condition, not an acute one. Besides, myriad ways existed to try to avoid the army and jail, and many or most of us had hope, if not faith, that we would find one.

Many of *us? Us?*

Not poor whites from Appalachia or poor blacks from inner-city slums or poor Puerto Ricans from the barrio, whose poverty or lack of education made college and a 2-S student deferment impossible. Those young men either were drafted and shipped to Vietnam with no questions asked, or they saw the draft coming and the army as their route out of poverty and second-class citizenship and volunteered. In the end, the result was the same. Race and class determined who lived and who died. To the Selective Service System, all men were not created equal.

The spring of 1970 at Antioch College, with its bucolic campus and 1000-acre nature preserve called Glen Helen, featured the expected protests and polemics. At the entrance to the Student Union, the Young Socialist Alliance maintained a bulletin board with a poster that showed a factory belching black smoke into the air with the caption "Capitalism Pollutes."

That quarter I was studying and reading a lot: for my course in educational theory (I thought I might want to be a teacher), books with titles like *Teaching As a Subversive Activity* and *Education and Ecstasy*, as well as A.S. Neill's *Summerhill* and John Holt's *How Children Fail*; and, for my course in Depression era literature, works by Dos Passos, Faulkner, and Nathaniel West.

One evening my friend Nelson and I concocted the idea of submitting to the dean a proposal for a project we tentatively titled "Studies In Leisure Time Activities." We'd build a model train system that would run throughout the entire Student Union building—with tunnels through the walls, trestles in the hallways, and tracks running above the stairs suspended from the ceilings. Although initially enthusiastic, ultimately we despaired. In our hearts we knew that even for anything-goes Antioch, our train proposal was bound not for glory but for rejection—not because the idea was totally nuts, but rather because it would cost too much.

All in all, the campus was relatively peaceful. Until April 30.

That day Dick Nixon announced the invasion—he called it an "incursion"—into Cambodia. America's colleges, including Antioch, erupted with demonstrations and vigils, takeovers of buildings, and demands that colleges and universities shut down so that students, faculty, and staff could work full-time to end the war. Student leaders called for a national student strike.

Four days later, on May 4 at Kent State University, a three-and-a-half hour drive from Yellow Springs, the Ohio National Guard fired sixty-seven rounds from their semi-automatic weapons at peace demonstrators, killing four—Allison Krause, Jeffrey Miller, William Schroeder, and Sandra Scheuer—and wounding nine more. The response was fierce. More campuses closed down. Demonstrations ran rampant. Before Kent State, "Bring The War Home" had been one of the slogans of the anti-war movement. The killings at that campus indeed brought the war home, but on the government's terms, not ours. The irony was palpable.

And so was the fear. Some days and hours I felt energized, optimistic and hopeful, but often I felt overwhelmed by a sense of dread.

For some weeks or months, I held onto the belief that the anti-war resistance, the protests and demonstrations and denunciations of Nixon, the draft-card burnings, the induction refusals—all put together—might actually end the war. But by the time colleges reopened in the fall of 1970, the anti-war fervor had wilted, and the war in Vietnam had continued and was continuing unabated.

The conflagration would continue for five more years. Before America's military misadventure finally ended—with helicopters evacuating our soldiers and other American personnel off the roof of the United

States embassy in the city then called Saigon, over 20,000 more Americans and a million more Vietnamese would die in the carrion horror of that conflict.

A friend, Cora Kaplan, who graduated from Smith College in 1961 (and later would become a professor of English literature at Rutgers, the University of London, Southampton University and Queen Mary College), tells the story of being present in 1962 in New York City at the creation of the drafts of the Port Huron Statement. The Port Huron Statement was to the New Left what the Declaration of Independence was to American colonists—the manifesto of the movement, a diatribe of grievances, a call for action. The drafts were written, distributed, and debated at the Students for a Democratic Society (SDS) office on East 19th Street in Manhattan. The thoughts and words of Tom Hayden and some other guys needed to be typed onto purple-inked master sheets for a ditto machine from which, in that pre-photocopying age, multiple copies could be made. That job was assigned to Cora, a twenty-two-year-old "girl," as they would refer to her. The movement was sexist.

Ray Mungo, a founder of the Liberation News Service (LNS) and author of *Famous Long Ago* (the title being lifted from Dylan's "Desolation Row"), honed his craft as a writer and journalist at the *Boston University News* and LNS. To the anti-war movement, Ray Mungo mattered. Many people looked up to him, respected his views, his energy and talent. Notwithstanding that, Mungo—who was and is gay—could not even imagine the possibility that he could come out. The movement was homophobic.

Another criticism: although I felt at the time that I was devotedly fighting to end the war, in reality, mostly what I did was sit in meetings, march in demonstrations, and write to elected officials letters that were sufficiently angry and vitriolic so as to guarantee they would never be answered. In retrospect, these activities appear insignificant.

A final caveat: My generation, as depicted in the media anyway, was supposed to be joyous, hedonistic—sex, drugs, rock'n'roll, the Age of Aquarius, Woodstock, and all that. In truth, joy often felt in short supply, and I, like many others, lived with an undercurrent of fatalism. I wrote the initial iteration of the Kent State piece in this book shortly after the killings there. One night, in anticipation of a demonstration the next day where, we had been warned, the police might smash our heads and legs, and afraid that Kent State meant that law enforcement could now kill long-haired, anti-war college kids with impunity, I wrote, "Everyone could write a book. I wrote mine early to make sure it got done."

And yet:

The antiwar agitation of the 1960s and early 1970s, the demonstrations and denunciations of governmental power, our refusal to accept the carnage of the war, and our antipathy towards the warmakers—all that empowered us. Our collective disdain of the too powerful, our revulsion at their cavalierly killing young people, and our belief that out of the chaos we could make something better—these principles unified us.

However vaguely the movement might be defined, quite unintentionally I had become part of something bigger and more important than myself. We celebrated the lack of definition as part of a process of discovery. As Buffalo Springfield's lyrics put it, "There's something happening here/what it is ain't exactly clear."

My metamorphosis occurred at Antioch, the college I attended because of an off-hand remark by the college guidance counselor at Hotchkiss, the prep school I attended for four years. He didn't like me and had particular disdain for my lack of school spirit, apparently demonstrated by my insufficient enthusiasm in rooting for the varsity football team and my excessive interest in writing poems for the literary magazine. At our mandatory meeting, trying to be diplomatic, I asked him for suggestions about college, and he replied, "Well, a place like Antioch might want someone like you."

Before that meeting I had never heard of Antioch, but that sentence reverberated in my mind. I believed then that some colleges would admit me, but it had never occurred to me that some college might actually *want* me—Hotchkiss so obviously didn't. After reading about its work-study program and how demonstrations by students in the 1950s had integrated the local barber-shop, and learning that Antioch was the first college in the country to admit women as students and to hire women faculty on an equal basis with men, and that Coretta Scott King and Rod Serling were graduates, I couldn't fill out the application fast enough.

Antioch accepted me in December 1967. I never applied anywhere else and didn't see the campus until the day I arrived as a freshman in the summer of 1968. (Antioch operated twelve months a year—with half the students on campus, and the other half away on a work quarter.) That fall I began working for the Vera Institute's Court Employment Project.

At Vera, I began to seriously learn about race, class, and privilege, but as my compromises with the draft demonstrated, not so seriously that I felt compelled to shunt aside hypocrisy and resolve the contradictions between the beliefs I professed to hold and my status as a beneficiary of a system rigged in my favor. Publicly proclaiming my beliefs was one thing. Voluntarily relinquishing all privileges—that was something else altogether. Near the top of the list of benefits: maybe, hopefully, by the time I completed college, the war would be over and the draft abolished.

Given these kinds of inherent inconsistencies and myriad other factors, it should surprise no one that the student anti-war movement did not revolutionize America. I still marvel at the depth of our conviction at that time that it would.

And we did help accomplish something. As Bobby Kennedy put it, "Every time a man stands up for an ideal, or acts to improve the lot of others, or strikes out against injustice, he sends forth a tiny ripple of hope, and those ripples build a current which can sweep down the mightiest walls of oppression and resistance." The continued fight for racial and gender equality, LGBT rights, and the environment, it seems to me, constitute proof of our commitment. For most of us who lived through that time, the movement endures. It endures for me, more than anything else, in the lives of our daughters.

Hotchkiss, when I was there, was an all-boys school. I never had a girl as a friend (or a girlfriend for that matter) until college. But at Antioch, equality was more than accepted—it was imbedded in the ethos of the institution. On campus no one really questioned the goals of the women's movement although, to be honest, at times I utterly failed to understand the adamancy. I remember arguing with a woman student who took umbrage at my adhering to, she insisted, traditional gender roles when I held a door open for her. And after four years of a New England boys' boarding school, it took time for me to not evaluate all interactions with women in terms of the possibility of sex. (Plus, it was the 1960s—there was that possibility.)

That said, I worked with women students in classes, on theatre projects, and at co-op jobs, where I sometimes had women supervisors. And I have fond memories of a woman friend, with more patience than I can now fathom, explaining how and why she was liberated enough to wear a bra. I entered Antioch as a sexist Neanderthal, but in a way I kind of grokked that, and over time the idea of women not being at least the equal of men evolved into a foreign concept. My falling in love with a woman personally and politically committed to the women's movement sealed the deal.

In April 1995, for the twenty-fifth anniversary of the Kent State shootings, I turned "Kent State, Glen Helen, and the Strike" into a piece that appeared in *Hampshire Life*, the weekly magazine of the *Daily Hampshire Gazette* newspaper, published in my hometown, Northampton, Massachusetts. The cover of the magazine reproduced the iconic Pulitzer Prize–winning photograph of Mary Ann Vecchio screaming as she knelt by the body of Jeffrey Miller, whom the National Guard had just shot and killed at Kent State. The magazine gave the article a new title, "When the War Came Home."

From January 1995 through November 2002, I also wrote a monthly column for that newspaper. My relationship with the editor experienced some ups and downs. I once found myself in hot water for writing a piece chiding the paper (this was pre-spell-check) about its chronic typos. "We're not paying you [thirty dollars per column] to criticize the paper," I was admonished.

Exacerbating my in-the-doghouse status, the next month I submitted a column that began by describing porn star Annie Sprinkle's cervix. "Don't you know this is a family newspaper?" I was chastised yet again. (More about this at page 202.) However, my occasional spats with the powers-that-be at the paper did not cause me to stop writing for it. Rather, I gave up writing columns when composing them began to feel driven more by inertia and less by inspiration or outrage.

In 2013, after a hiatus of more than a decade, the Gazette's editor, a different editor, asked if I would like my column back and, feeling energized anew, I said yes. But before beginning, I wanted to try to understand what had worked in those earlier pieces and what hadn't. To that end I exhumed them from boxes in a closet in my office and began reading.

The columns, I found, had been eclectic, with topics ranging from abortion, boomers, wiretapping, and free speech to political races, murder trials, legal services, gay rights, and criminal justice issues, including prominently—and probably because during those years I was representing a man on Georgia's death row—capital punishment. Many mused about my family, especially my daughters, who were teenagers then.

Culling the columns and other pieces I had written during those years made me realize that a number of them still lived. That awareness for me changed the question from what works? to what lasts? and its corollary, why?

Many of the pieces that had lasted, I came to see, share as their lodestar the tumult of the 1960s and early 1970s and my experience of being part of that movement, no matter its shortcomings and failings and my extremely modest contributions. Those stories, grounded in that experience, at least try, in the words of the author and poet Patricia Schneider, to "build from the fragments of our lives/maps to guide us to each other." Those pieces are this book.

At Antioch my other co-op jobs (what today we'd call a paid internship) were teaching at a preschool (where I loved the head teacher and learned a lot, including that I probably lacked the patience to do that job well over a long time); working as an editorial assistant for *TransPacific*, a literary magazine (where I did the initial read and felt perennially paranoid that I had just placed a piece from the next Saul Bellow back in the slush pile); and writing press releases and doing other public relations work at the Urban Law Institute in Washington (which was embroiled in a lawsuit against the major banks for their having red-lined the black neighborhoods of D.C. as ineligible for home loans).

I had known, of course, that attending Antioch and opposing the war in Vietnam had shaped my professional and personal life. Rereading those pieces made me appreciate how much those experiences had changed me.

Antioch, which made me value how much I learned by not being ensconced in classrooms, motivated me to attend law school at Northeastern University, which operates on a similar model of cooperative education with alternating quarters of work and study. While in law school, I worked for two small civil rights and criminal defense law firms, one in Boston, the other in Springfield, Massachusetts. At both I investigated facts, drafted motions, and assisted at counsel table for a first-degree– murder trial. For another co-op, I traveled to the Rio Grande Valley to work for Texas Rural Legal Aid, where I represented farmworkers in unemployment, Social Security, and welfare hearings. For another work quarter I moved to Anchorage, where, as an employee of the Alaska Public Defenders Agency, I drafted three briefs for the state supreme court.

In total I spent eight years on co-op plans and, after law school, couldn't quite give up that life. For the four months between taking the bar exam and receiving the results, I lived on the Menominee Indian reservation in Wisconsin working for the Warrior Society. (Some of my experiences on "the rez" are included in the section of this book titled "Jew Boy.")

In preparation for publication, I've edited almost all the pieces—some a little; others, a lot. There is good precedent for editing already published writing, and we lawyers like precedent—at least when it favors us. Accordingly, I hereby cite Sylvia Plath, who, even after poems of hers had been published, would nonetheless continue to rework and rewrite them. As far as she was concerned, the published poem was not necessarily the finished poem. Rather, it was the poem as it was at that time.

An exception to this paradigm of revision is "Radio Wars," a magazine feature that I coauthored with my daughter Leah when she was thirteen. I didn't want to futz with the writing there for fear of altering the voices with which we spoke to each other then.

Looking back, I have few regrets about these pieces. I'm grateful for the chance to have worked on them again. I wish I had written more about my mom.

KENT STATE, GLEN HELEN, AND THE 1970 NATIONAL STUDENT STRIKE

From the *Antioch College Bulletin*, 1969–1970

*Be ashamed to die until you have won some victory
for humanity.*
— Horace Mann, President, Antioch College,
Farewell Address, 1884

*Antioch's purpose is to equip college students to live
effectively in a complex and changing world....*

*The college's plan of cooperative education requires
students to alternate quarters of study and work....*

*The main campus borders Glen Helen, the college's
thousand acre nature preserve in Yellow Springs, Ohio.*

May 1

From my pine-needle seat in Glen Helen, I hear the sound of a faraway train traveling on the night currents in the stillness that just precedes the dawn. With the first streaks of light, I close my eyes. But the sky becomes brighter and the day warmer. It is time to leave.

I walk up the stone steps out of the Glen, across Corry Street, past the Student Union. From the radio reports the night before I know the headlines that are splashed on the newspapers that students are reading on the stoop of the Union. *United States Invades Cambodia.*

I shake my head. I want to know: Won't this ever end?

We're slaughtering the people of Vietnam and now Cambodia, defoliating the countryside with Agent Orange, and searing farmers and children with napalm. GIs my age cut off the ears of the people they've killed to confirm body counts, to prove we're winning the war. They bury the ears or fingers that they've cut off a Vietcong boy only after the gaseous smell gets too nauseating to bear. The secretaries of defense, first Robert McNamara, now Melvin Laird, say we will have won that war once we've counted a certain number of bodies, but they refuse to say how many.

May 2

The New York Times: President Nixon referred today to campus radicals who oppose his Vietnam policies as bums, in contrast to American soldiers, whom he called "the greatest."

> *TheAntioch Record:* The Antioch faculty voted almost unanimously "against all U.S. intervention in Southeast Asia...." The words at the beginning of the resolution, "Antioch College takes an institutional stand against," were replaced with the [words] "The Antioch faculty stands against...."

MEMORANDUM

TO: James P. Dixon, President
              Antioch College

FROM: Bill Newman

DATE: May 2, 1970

SUBJECT: Strike Demand

There has been a lot of talk in the last forty-eight hours about what it would mean for Antioch College to take an institutional stand against the war. Most of this talk has been wasted rhetoric and stupid slogans.

The concept of academic freedom, it seems to me, does not include passive acceptance of our government's senseless and illegal killing and maiming of a million or more innocent people in a war that we cannot win and should not fight. What complicates this so much for you, for us?

We are supposed to be a community so let's be one and as a community, take our stand against this war and do everything possible to stop it. We should start today by hoisting a huge banner on the Student Union building that says, "ANOTHER FAMILY FOR PEACE."

MEMORANDUM

TO: Richard Nixon, President
     United States of America

FROM: Bill Newman

DATE: May 2, 1970

SUBJECT: War

You were correct when you said that you will not be the first president to lose a war. Rather, you will be remembered for presiding over a horrible end to a horrible war. But don't despair, for your distinction in history will be greater than this. You may be remembered as the first president to lose America.

* * *

I know that Nixon doesn't pay any attention to what I have to say or the words of anyone like me for that matter. There's a certain equipoise here because I don't pay too much attention to what Nixon has to say. I take that back—actually, I do pay attention to his words. I just don't believe any of them.

Some politician should halt Nixon's insidious games, but McGovern can't win, Muskie has no voice, and Kennedy drinks and drives.

May 4

Evening News: *The Ohio National Guard shot their semi-automatics into a crowd of anti-war student protesters at Kent State University, killing four. Nine others were wounded; three are in critical condition*

May 5

Morning

This morning I could not tell
what was sleep
and what was not.

I heard the dawn
crawl away,

dogs lap up the fog.
Fists rubbed
my eyes madras, open

as dreams
cut through
the windows.

I was afraid
to get up, to see blood
drying on the panes.

Afternoon

There was a protest in downtown Yellow Springs. The "STRIKE-EXTRA" edition of *The Antioch Record*, reported that *The march... brought a handful of people to the entrances of stores to smile, wave, or make obscene gestures....*

May 6

All day my stomach has felt like I've been riding on the tilt-a-whirl at Playland, a ride that, when I was eight or nine years old, always put me on the verge of throwing up. I went on it only because my friends did, and afterwards fantasized about diving into a cold pool. But Playland had no pool, only concrete. Just thinking about it makes me taste the vomit that I managed to squelch then.

I know where this queasiness comes from: Nixonites are killing college kids. We said that they could, or they might, or they would, but at Kent State they really are doing it.

The government claims a sniper was shooting at the National Guardsmen, who justifiably shot back, but camera crews filmed the whole demonstration. There was no sniper. The National Guard simply opened fire. Unbelievable.

Detesting Nixon, Agnew, and Westmoreland—all of them—has become second nature. But now what?

A poster of Che Guevara, the Argentine Marxist physician, author, and revolutionary, is hanging near the entrance to the college bookstore. At the bottom is his quote: "At the risk of sounding ridiculous, let me say that the true revolutionary is guided by feelings of great love."

Fine. Great. But Che is dressed in army fatigues, holding a machine gun with bullets draped over him. How the fuck does that message fit with my conscientious objector application that still sits, I assume, in some file cabinet at my draft board?

May 7

> **News report:** *Demonstrations against the war and protests against the deaths at Kent State continue along with plans for the demonstration in Washington.*

Morning

People are screaming all sorts of revolutionary rhetoric, words that seemed totally crazy—at least until this week. They are screaming that a revolution is coming and you either are for it or against it, it's time to get in or get out. I feel so lost. A classmate accused me of suffering from lingering liberalism. She made it sound like a disease.

Evening

We met for hours in North Hall about the demonstrations planned for Columbus, Ohio, and Washington, D.C. Lots of logistics: where to park, where to stay, numbers to call for medical aid, for legal help if they start busting people; the signs, the slogans; how to deal with the nightsticks, some self-defense training. By the time the meeting was over, it was very late, but no one felt tired.

We ended up in the parking lot. Some folks brought guitars and played protest songs and Beatles tunes. The scene reminded me of the advice Allen Ginsberg gave at a poetry reading at Antioch in the summer of 1968. When asked how we could best try to explain ourselves to the older generation, Ginsberg answered, "By singing, dancing, and fucking."

Getting laid. Now there's one terrific idea, but Wendy, who I want to be doing that with, is on a co-op job in Washington and besides, as I need to keep reminding myself, she has broken up with me at least twice.

In the parking lot you could feel the unspoken understanding that we all would be standing together tomorrow when it mattered at the demonstration—what the government likes to label a conspiracy. I wonder, could our gathering in the parking lot get us all indicted? What with the singing and dancing and smoking pot, the evidence is building.

May 8

At the march and demonstration in Columbus, I was a marshal. For two hours the police and state troopers guarded the flag, and we guarded them. They had guns and Mace and clubs. We had black armbands and buttons and NBC News.

After arriving at the capitol grounds a debate raged among the protesters, then ebbed and flowed. Could we, should we, try to storm the capitol building in order to get inside, to get to the cupola, to get to the American flag flying above it, to lower it to half-staff, where, dammit, it belongs? How many people would be hurt and how badly? And could we actually get inside?

Cooler heads did not exactly prevail. But the building was surrounded by police, and the people who were advocating trying to stampede our way inside didn't seem all that convinced that we should and after a while, gave up that idea.

When the rally ended, we guarded the cops until the last of our people had left. We said "Good-bye. And Peace." They all looked tired, having stood in the sun, wearing heavy riot gear, for a long time. We were glad to see them looking hot and tired, in addition to dangerous.

> *The Antioch Record,* **May 8, 1970:** *The march on Columbus this afternoon was reported "peaceful and quiet" at press time.*

> Caption on picture: *THE UNITED STATES FLAG flies at one-quarter staff this week at Antioch in mourning for four Kent State University students....*

> *Across the nation nearly 425 colleges have student strikes ... Ohio ... Illinois ... New York ... Michigan ...Massachusetts.... Faculties have called for the impeachment of President Nixon and Vice President Agnew....*

May 9

A long night on I-70 East to D.C., but I was feeling good for the dawn.

We drove alongside VW buses filled with people who looked like us and exchanged Vs and clenched fists.

Every time we saw a state trooper we felt nervous and looked the other way or at each other or at the floor or the dashboard. Anti-war bumper stickers and state troopers don't mix well, and guys with long hair make it all worse.

Long hair for a guy tends to restrict travel to north of the Mason-Dixon line, east of the Appalachians, or west of the Sierra Nevadas. This is too bad. The Constitution used to guarantee free travel between the states, and I used to believe in the Constitution, among other things. And besides, Antioch is in southwest Ohio.

Two Stories In The Car

At a demonstration in front of the Century Plaza Hotel in Los Angeles thousands of demonstrators had massed to meet Vice President Hubert Humphrey. The fountains were overflowing with soap bubbles because someone had tossed Salvo tablets in them, and the demonstrators as a whole were in a relatively jovial mood, popping the bubbles and shouting insults at Hubie.

Until the cops started shoving the demonstrators and ordering them to move back. The demonstrators yelled that they couldn't unless the thousands behind them moved first.

The cops screamed through an improvised loudspeaker system, "We order you in the name of the people of Los Angeles County and the State of California to turn back and disperse." And the demonstrators, who actually had secured a parade permit, roared back, "We are the people. We are the people." Some, of course, were screaming at the cops, "Fuck you," and "Off the pigs," but not too many.

* * *

Michael told us a story about UNDO, a group headquartered at Princeton. UNDO, short for the Group to Undo the Draft.

UNDO's theory runs something like this: The Selective Service System (SSS) is a bureaucracy of the worst sort, a military bureaucracy. Accordingly, it is not only crass, corrupt, and inhuman, but also incredibly inefficient. It follows rules, no matter how inane they might be; indeed, the rules have a life of their own. The SSS doesn't really draft people to send to Southeast Asia to die or have their legs blown off (that might even upset a few of the people who work there). All the SSS does is follow rules. This creates opportunity for a group like UNDO.

According to UNDO, SSS regulations both require draft boards to answer every written question from a registrant about his draft status and prevent an induction order from being issued to anyone who has an inquiry outstanding. Michael heard of an UNDO guy who daily writes his draft board a letter which begins, "Deardraftboard:Iamwritingyout hisletterregardingmydraftstatus.Ihaveanimportantquestion.Iamsorrythatthespacebaronmytypewriterisbroken."

And his draft board has started to answer each one.

Arrival

We arrived in D.C. and went to Wendy's apartment. She opened the door and didn't kiss me hello.

Her place was crowded with folks sleeping on the floor. For one moment, I closed my eyes and was back in Yellow Springs with her, hearing the calls of thrushes and the cawing of crows and smelling the plum and apple blossoms. For a moment I could touch the time we spent together. For a moment.

Back to reality: Wendy made some coffee, but said she couldn't stay for even a few minutes—that she was a marshal for the march and had to leave for a staging area. I told her she didn't need to leave right then, and added that I'd probably spend the summer in Yellow Springs for a study quarter and asked her if she would be coming back to school. She said she really liked working in D.C., would be staying there for another quarter, and, anyway, had sort of met somebody. After she left, closing the door softly, I felt the way I usually do when she leaves—incredibly alone.

After a while, the rest of us who had caravanned together from Yellow Springs trooped off toward the march to find the Ohio contingent. We passed a drugstore called "People's Drugs." Someone began a riff about D.C. being a fine place, perhaps the politicians are misunderstood, what other city would openly admit to "People's Drugs?"

And the people kept coming and coming. There must have been a million of us. Chanting slogans. Demanding peace. Screaming at Nixon to fuck off.

At the Ellipse we swayed together in long snake-dance lines, singing, "All we are saying is give peace a chance." John Lennon's voice in our heads, "All we are saying is give peace a chance."

May 10

> **News item:** *Yesterday Nixon made a pre-dawn visit to the Lincoln Memorial where protestors were camped. Two Syracuse University students commented, "Most of what he was saying was absurd... (our) university (is) completely uptight, on strike, and when we told him where we were from, he talked about the football team. And when someone said he was from California, he talked about surfing."*

At the march, poets read and singers sang.

Robert Bly's poem "The Teeth Mother Naked at Last" says, "The Marines use cigarette lighters to light the thatched roofs of huts because so many Americans own their own homes." Homeowning is the quintessential American dream. So why do we treat Vietnamese homes as worthless straw, valueless except as fuel for bonfires? I want to know: Who gave Johnson and Nixon the right to make the Vietnamese version of the American dream a nightmare of women and children screaming as their flesh burns inside those thatched huts? Did they pay no attention when Martin Luther King said that racism at home and imperialism abroad are the flip sides of the same coin?

At the rally Dave Dellinger, the famous pacifist and a revolutionary, made a great speech. He is facing seven-and-a-half years in prison thanks to Judge Julius Hoffman—five for demonstrating at the Democratic National Convention and another two-and-a-half for refusing to act obsequiously toward the judge at his trial.

Dellinger must be close to forty years old, which makes me think that this never-trust-a-person-over-thirty thing really is only a media invention. While Abbie Hoffman, Jerry Rubin, Dave Dellinger, William Kunstler, Gene McCarthy, and George McGovern all have passed that chronological milestone, most undercover narcs are longhairs in their twenties. Being thirty doesn't mean anything more than being thirty, and scientists studying the aging process dispute it even means that.

May 11

Nixon likes to summarize things on legal pads. His list for invading Cambodia was longer than his list for not.

I have my own list, a list of reasons for hating Nixon's America, a list with a lot of death on it: John F. Kennedy, Robert F. Kennedy, Martin Luther King, Jr.; Malcolm X, Medgar Evers; Andrew Goodman, Michael Schwerner, James Chaney; Allison Krause, Jeffrey Miller, William Schroeder, Sandra Scheuer. My list grows longer. How about 30,000 American servicemen? How about a million Vietnamese?

May 12

There are pictures in my mind so vivid they could be framed on my desk: Jack Ruby shooting Lee Harvey Oswald in the basement of the Dallas police station, Oswald doubling over, the fat Texas state trooper with the ten-gallon hat cringing as the gun goes off; the photograph of the South Vietnamese general holding his gun to the head of a teenage boy, a suspected Vietcong, just before he blows that boy's brains out; the picture of the naked Vietnamese girl crying, screaming, running down the middle of the dirt road away from the fighting and killing and napalm, while the soldiers and peasants trudge numbly along.

Now there is another: the picture of a young woman with dark hair, Mary Anne Vecchio, hysterical and screaming, kneeling beside the body of Kent State student Jeffrey Miller, shot dead by the Ohio National Guard.

Allison Krause's father spoke a simple truth: This didn't have to happen.

Through tears, another father of another shot-dead Kent State student, responding to President Nixon's characterization of protestors, said, "My daughter was not a bum."

May 15

The New York Times, **page 1:** *Military officials announced that 803 South Vietnamese soldiers were killed last week...American losses—168 killed and 1001 wounded—were the highest in eight months. North Vietnamese and Vietcong losses were put at 5898....*

Jackson, Mississippi... [At a demonstration] a barrage of police gunfire left two students dead, James Earl Green, 17, a senior and star miler on the track team, and Phillip L. Green, 21, a junior....Police say there was a sniper....

* * *

Back in the darkroom I printed photographs that I had taken on a sweltering summer day in July 1968 at the Republican Governors' Conference in Cincinnati. Protesters were picketing the conference. Familiar signs: Stop the Killing, Stop the War. Rednecks and construction workers were yelling *faggot—hippie—commie—asshole* at the protesters and threatening to beat the shit out of the anti-war demonstrators.

Image after image on negatives of governors arriving for their gala evening dinner. When presidential candidate Governor George Romney and his wife, Lenore, walked by, she noticed my camera and instantaneously smiled, right into the lens. I got the Romneys—perhaps a valuable picture if he hadn't later used the word "brainwashed" to describe what the military brass did when selling him the virtues of the war, a statement that effectively ended his quest for the White House.

Next roll of film: some Nixon campaign workers marching by. Straw hats with red, white, and blue bunting—I remember. A woman, maybe twenty, glaring at the protesters—and me. Her face, filled with disdain, looking straight at me, emerging slowly in black and white on the paper in the bottom of the developing tray.

More images: Ronald and Nancy Reagan walking by—smiling and laughing, affable in front of television crews, on their way to shrimp cocktail, fine wine, and roast tenderloin. Snapped Reagan. A fine photograph. Black-striped collar on his off-white tuxedo jacket. Sun at my back. Good framing of him, thanks to TV news cameras between us on my left and right.

On the bulletin board in the Student Union, next to the picture of the factory belching smoke, someone has posted a quote from Reagan, a statement he made shortly before Kent State about ending student violence: "If it takes a bloodbath, let's get it over with." When asked later if he meant it, he called his statement "a figure of speech."

May 16

After a teach-in on the wartime economy, my friend Helen and I went out to the farm that lets us ride their horses. Our horse-back riding is supposed to count toward a PE credit, which we actually don't need anymore since the strike will continue for the rest of the quarter and the college has already announced that it will either give us the credit or waive the requirement.

For about two hours we rode in the pine forest near the Glen, where we saw two red-winged blackbirds and luxuriated under a deep blue sky and the warm spring sun.

When we returned to the barn, the news was on the radio, and the war was on the news. The announcer said allied forces were continuing to invade Cambodia. Something called Operation Total Victory. It also said America had begun bombing North Vietnam again. That apparently had no fancy military title and was simply called Bombing North Vietnam. Again.

I fed the horse some extra oats. He seemed content enough.

May 17

In step with the darkness the drummer plays on. Play on, drummer, play on. Play on, drummer, play on. Play for the revolution. Play with this tired darkness. Play for the revolution. Play on, drummer, play on. Streaks appear in the sky and thin rattles play on. Play on, drummer, play on. Play to announce the revolution. Or at least the coming of dawn.

May 20

Stoned! We talked about how it must feel to be a letter. Do A and Z have a perspective vastly different from the others? Do Cs and Ms and Ws feel fat? Does W feel cozy surrounded by all those letters or badly that she's always so near the end?

Talking about words gave us the idea for a publication. We got this far: the *Freaky Bi-Weekly* would have words, pictures, and pages, and on the masthead we'd put a dedication to Panama Red.

At midnight we went to the bakery for freshly baked hot donuts and chocolate milk. God, those donuts tasted delicious! We each devoured four or five and gulped a quart of chocolate milk, too.

May 21

In the light of day, it turns out that the *Freaky Bi-Weekly* would take a lot of work and that the words of the title don't exactly rhyme.

August 16

> **News item:** *The National Student Association voted 150 to 134 against a plan for a massive demonstration in Washington, D.C., to close the city down if all American troops were not pulled out of Vietnam by May 1971. It committed itself instead to concerted, expanded, nonviolent action including civil disobedience.*

Dick Nixon on the radio, Dick Nixon on television, Dick Nixon in newspapers. Listening to Nixon makes revolution sound awfully good, maybe even inevitable. A lot of people at a lot of meetings have been saying that. When I woke up this morning I looked outside for the revolution, but all I saw was the mailman. He handed me a flyer. At our local IGA supermarket, there is a special on hamburger.

October 14

The facts are out: As everyone already knew, there was no sniper at Kent State. The National Guard was never in danger. So what happened?

The Ohio Grand Jury absolved the National Guard from blame for the four deaths. According to the government, the guardsmen shot—I guess they don't like the word murdered—in the honest belief that they were in danger—although no one can identify that danger. The official report concludes that the "major responsibility for the deaths lies with the university administrators who fostered permissiveness and over-emphasized the right to dissent."

There we have it—the government's version of truth. Follow the bouncing logic: No sniper existed at Kent State, and the demonstrators were armed with only words, banners, and conviction. But the National Guard might have been afraid of some sniper who could have existed but didn't, and therefore they justifiably shot and killed defenseless people.

This passes for justice? Can you imagine what would have happened if anti-war demonstrators had shot and killed four National Guardsmen?

October 15

We were afraid of a bust and climbed up into the attic through the top of the closet to hide an ounce. There was nothing in the attic—not even fear.

January 19, 1971

> **News report:** *Defense Secretary Melvin Laird defended the widened U.S. air role in Cambodia this week as crucial to the success of Nixon's Vietnamization of the war policy. North Vietnam charged that American bombers for the past two weeks have been flying daily defoliation missions. The Pentagon says that the bombing was "protective-reaction" strikes over the Ho Chi Minh Trail in Laos. Senator Majority Leader Mike Mansfield says that "the sounds of war in Indochina again are growing ominous."*

I took a walk in Glen Helen, a place I love. It's a magic sanctuary. But with all the cacophony and hatred in the world I can't go there anymore and try to be peaceful in that peaceful place.

As I was leaving, at the top of the stone stairs, I looked back into the Glen, not wanting to say goodbye. And in a way, I suppose I didn't. No one really says goodbye to the Glen because everyone hopes to return some day.

Postscript: The Draft

On the fifth day after my eighteenth birthday (the Selective Service Law required you to register within five days of turning eighteen), I entered an office in a basement of a building in Springfield, Ohio, that was weirdly quiet, had almost no furniture, and only one person, a woman, fifty or sixty, in the room sitting behind a desk.

I said, "I just turned eighteen," and she replied, "So you want to register."

"Name, full name ... what do you mean you only have a middle initial? How can you only have a middle initial? Birthdate, place of birth, identifying characteristics, address, ... someone who will always know where you are, ... you'll get a form in the mail." I checked the box saying I was a full-time student. The Selective Service System sent me a draft card and another card, a classification—2-S, my student deferment. To the Selective Service System I was #50/7/50/250.

On December 2, 1969, the day after the first draft lottery, the one that assigned me my place in the queue, I went to the college library, having heard that the results were posted on a bulletin board near the entrance. They were. Every date of the year was listed, 1 through 366, in three columns: 1 through 122 (the left-hand column); 123 through 244 (the middle column); 245 through 366 (the column on the right).

I started at the bottom of the right-hand column—at 366. When my index finger came to number 300, I took a breath. After all, you were absolutely safe from the draft if you had a number over 200, so I had a long way to go.

After not finding my birthdate in the right-hand column, I started at the bottom of the middle one and once again moved my finger slowly up the page. When I came to 200 and still hadn't found August 8, I paused briefly. Relax, I told myself. I had heard that if your birthday had a number above 150, you most probably would never receive an induction notice, and number 125 could constitute the actual cut-off point, depending on how many bodies the army needed in the year of your eligibility.

My finger arrived at number 150 without seeing my birthdate, then 125. I considered starting over at 366 in case I'd overlooked my birthdate, but instead slowly pushed my finger up the left-hand column. Eventually I came to my birthdate. The number next to it was 48.

I trudged away from the library, desperately wanting someone to talk to, but I didn't have a close friend on campus that quarter. It was a clear, beautiful day and one of the loneliest afternoons of my life.

After receiving my draft lottery number, there wasn't much for me to do about the draft—except wait. Because of the work–study program, the SSS had designated Antioch as a five-year, instead of a four-year, college, so I planned to stay enrolled for five full years, through June 1973. Then, on December 30, 1971, while on an end-of-the-year break, I saw on the front page of *The New York Times* a headline that read, "Thousands of Young Men May Escape Draft." I couldn't get the fifteen cents out of my pocket fast enough.

The paper reported that Secretary of Defense Melvin Laird had announced the suspension of draft calls in January and February. The story said draft calls could resume in March, but some experts thought they wouldn't.

The article explained that, because of recent changes in the law, men were subject to the draft for only one year. The year could be extended—but only once—and only for three more months. That was it. After fifteen months, if Selective Service hadn't grabbed you, you were home free.

There was more.

Other regulations said that if a man classified 2-S applied for a 1-A (eligible for induction) classification, he was deemed classified 1-A as of the date—and for the year—of the postmark on the letter in which he requested the 1-A.

Putting all this together meant that if I mailed a letter to my draft board requesting 1-A status, postmarked on or before December 31, 1971, and the army didn't draft me by March 31, 1972, I had escaped. But if the draft did rev up again in March, given that lottery numbers 1 through 125 had already been called for induction in 1971, I—with my lottery number 48—literally would be standing at the front of that line.

That evening, Thursday, December 30, 1971, I wrote a letter to my draft board requesting a reclassification to 1-A status and the next day, Friday, December 31, hustled to the post office to mail it. I bought a stamp, put it on the envelope, went to the window, and handed it to a clerk who, maybe being in a rush to go home for New Year's Eve, tossed it into a big bin of mail without postmarking it.

Can you have a heart attack at age 21? Without the 1971 postmark, not only would I have voluntarily relinquished my deferment, but my letter also would have put me at the front of the line to be drafted for the next fifteen months, until March 31, 1973.

"Please. Can you please postmark that letter? Please."

"It'll be postmarked Monday, not to worry. It's not really moving much till then anyway."

"No, no really. I need it postmarked today. PLEASE."

The clerk glanced into the bin with the hundreds of pieces of mail and shrugged. My eyes were darting like a pinball in an arcade game, back and forth from the clerk to my letter. I was desperately trying to keep track of it as other clerks were tossing more mail into the bin, landing around and on top of it. The clerk in front of me looked skeptical and put upon. I feared he was about to tell me that the letter had been mailed, that he couldn't help me, and to get lost. After all, he was a middle-aged civil service post office employee, and I probably struck him as some long-haired hippie for whom he had no inclination to do any favors.

"This is about my not getting killed in Vietnam."

As soon as I said that, the panic churning inside me ratcheted up some more. What in God's name was I thinking? Maybe the clerk, looking at the kid in front of him, thought that my serving in the army and being sent to Vietnam was a fine idea. I pointed. "I can see it. It's that one." I kept pointing and jabbing through the air.

He turned to reach into the bin, pulled out an envelope, and asked, "This one?"

My heart sank.

"No, sir," I said and pointed again. But, of course, although I could still see it, to him I was pointing at hundreds of mostly indistinguishable envelopes, and maybe he was about to tell me that he had finished rummaging through them on my behalf. I tried to describe it as I pointed. He looked and reached in again.

"This one?"

I saw my handwriting and my draft board's address and said, "Yes. Yes. Yes. Thank you so much."

He then hand-stamped the letter and tossed it back into the bin. Two weeks later I received my new draft classification in the mail—1-A.

The army issued no draft calls in January or February, and also none in March. Draft calls resumed on April 1.

May 1995

THE WAR'S
AFTERMATH

FRIENDS WHO SERVED

As of April 30, 1975, the date America fled from Vietnam on helicopters from the roof of our embassy, 58,000 American soldiers had died in that war, and 150,000 more had been wounded. But for our soldiers the maiming and dying didn't stop. Afterwards, an untold number of Vietnam vets would commit suicide. Alcoholism, drug addiction, Agent Orange, and post traumatic stress killed others—less quickly, but with equal finality.

Vietnam vets never really could come home because the home they had left no longer existed. The war had changed them, and it had changed America, too. Shipped out as patriots, they returned to accusations that they were baby killers.

And some were. Our government measured military success by body counts, and the bodies of women and kids counted. As Tim O'Brien writes in *The Things They Carried*,

> *Lieutenant Cross carried his good-luck pebble. Dave Jensen, a rabbit's foot. Norman Bowker, otherwise a very gentle person, carried a thumb...dark brown, rubbery to the touch... cut from a [Vietcong] corpse, a boy of fifteen or sixteen.*

At the Veterans Education Project (VEP), headquartered in Amherst, Massachusetts, two dozen vets, all volunteers, use their stories to help teenagers escape the maelstrom of violence and drugs that cut short young lives, what VEP calls "The War at Home." These vets teach in high schools and middle schools, in classrooms and after-school programs and juvenile lockups, too. Trained by psychologists and educators, they do not preach. Rather, they tell stories—their stories.

*They carried the soldier's greatest fear, which was the
fear of blushing. Men killed and died because they
were embarrassed not to.*

Glenn Santos, 51, an administrator at an alternative middle school
in Springfield, talks about the day his helicopter was shot down and his
copilot and ten other soldiers were killed. Gordon Fletcher-Howell, an
owner of a landscape business, describes himself and his buddies search-
ing the area where they had returned fire and finding a small boy, perhaps eleven or twelve years old, lying next to a rifle, dead. Michael Har-
rington, a social worker, tells about his rescue mission near the Ho Chi
Minh trail that saved other soldiers' lives but cost him his right leg. At
one high school assembly, in front of all the students, he removed his
prosthesis and held it high to show the students one of the costs he bears
from Vietnam. These vets understand the losses that violence inflicts on
the victim—and the scars it leaves on the perpetrator, too.

*In addition to the three standard weapons—the M-60,
M-16, and M-79—they carried whatever presented
itself... as a means of killing or staying alive....They
carried all they could bear, and then some, including
a silent awe for the terrible power of the things they
carried.*

These vets understand the strange seduction of violence. It empow-
ers. Adrenaline flows. It infuses a feeling of near omnipotence. And the
consequences, as portrayed by television and movies, rarely amount to
anything at all.

*[A]ny solider will tell you, if he tells the truth... that
you're never more alive than when you're almost
dead.*

Decades after the Vietnam War ended, in some ways it still goes on.
For years, elected officials have attributed their positions about war and
peace to the lessons of Vietnam, lessons that apparently need to be relearned year after year, war after war.

*[F]or all the ambiguities of Vietnam, all the mysteries
and unknowns, there was at least the single abiding
certainty that they would never be at a loss of things
to carry....*

One evening, as I was standing in the dark parking lot of the Plain-ville Casting Company in Westfield, Massachusetts, the churning blades of a helicopter interrrupted my conversation with Dusty Houser, who made his living pouring molten metal at the foundry and also served as the union rep. As the helicopter approached, Dusty tensed noticeably, and I sensed him surveilling the area for someplace safe. "I hate those things. I hate what they bring back," Dusty told me. Dusty is a Vietnam vet.

My work as the foundry workers' lawyer has given me time to spend with Dusty. He and I talk about the war in spurts and starts, as I do with some of the men in the Veterans Education Project as well. From those conversations I take away this: If I had gone to Vietnam and lived, I don't believe I would have survived the war as well as they have. I don't think I would have the strength to carry what they carry. As Tim O'Brien writes, "They all carried ghosts."

October 2000

BOBBY
(On an Anniversary of His Assassination)

Funny how some things stick in your mind—the way the early morning of June 6, 1968, does in mine. I carry that moment with me like a Polaroid in my shirt pocket.

The war was raging in Southeast Asia, and a war against the war was raging in America. It was a time of discontent for the country but a contented time for me. Having received an early acceptance from Antioch College, I spent the spring mostly waiting for high school graduation.

Other young men were being shipped to Vietnam. A few of the kids in my class generally opposed the war and wanted to save soldiers' lives, but we actually didn't know anyone who had enlisted or been drafted. For my friends and me, college meant that we were protected from the draft for four or five years. By our next graduation, the war, no doubt, would be over. We felt safe.

On that June 6 morning, I could sense the sunlight sneaking around both sides of the shade and a warm breeze blowing. An India print spread covered my night table, and a black light hung in a corner—affectations in anticipation of college. After the clock-radio turned itself on, I lay in bed not even half-awake, waiting for the announcer to tell me the time so that I could squeeze in a few extra minutes of sleep. But he didn't give the time. Instead, the radio, it seemed, was repeatedly replaying news of President Kennedy's assassination.

Really weird programming, I thought. His birthday? This was no way to celebrate his birthday. The anniversary of the Dallas motorcade? No, that's November 22. I reached over to hit the snooze bar.

And then I bolted upright as if someone had slammed a steel rod through my spine. Because the radio wasn't rebroadcasting reports on Jack's assassination from 1963 or Martin Luther King's two months earlier. It was reporting on Bobby's the night before.

Today's politics makes it difficult, if not impossible, to explain Bobby to those who never experienced him. Robert Kennedy epitomized passion. People loved him. Or hated him. But everyone agreed on this: He was real. When Bobby condemned bigotry and vowed to fight racism, he meant it. As *New York Times* columnist Anthony Lewis once wrote, "The powerful feeling that he cared was sensed...by strangers—especially by the rejected of the earth who had no one else to care."

By 1968 cities had burned—and were still burning. Cargo planes were returning from Vietnam filled with body bags. The war, the killings, the riots made it feel as if an eternity had elapsed since President Kennedy had inspired us to "Ask not what your country can do for you, ask what you can do for your country."

For many of us President Kennedy was the first person to articulate idealism. Bobby made us feel that, despite everything that had happened, idealism still lived.

Bobby was a politician who, by the time he won the California primary, had paradoxically, in a sense, transcended politics. In his presidential campaign he did not move toward the center or compromise his views or muddy his convictions. To the contrary, he had become increasingly intolerant of intolerance. His Kennedy administration would have ended the war, and 30,000 Americans and a million Vietnamese would not have died needlessly at Nixon's direction.

Bobby's intensity and commitment captivated us. "Many politicians, perhaps most, become hardened or cynical over time," Anthony Lewis wrote. But Bobby, in contrast, "became warmer, more sympathetic, more understanding of humanity's imperfections." As the historian Arthur Schlesinger put it, "History changed him and, had time permitted, he might have changed history."

An eternal flame burns over President Kennedy's grave in Arlington National Cemetery but not over Bobby's. And just as well. An eternal flame over Bobby's grave would be false. When Sirhan Sirhan murdered him, something went out in America that has never been rekindled. That murder killed some, if not much, of the promise that Bobby embodied.

Instead of electing Bobby president in 1968, we ended up with Richard Nixon in the White House. Today, instead of reflections on RFK's presidency, we bear memories of the train carrying his body from New York to Washington, of another Kennedy in a flag-draped coffin, of the clanging of the train's funeral bell, of its melancholy whistle.

June 6, 1996

PROTEST AT GOODELL

A graduate student called me at my law office late one afternoon in March 1997 to convey a message from the protesters occupying Goodell Hall at the University of Massachusetts, Amherst. Could I come and give them some legal advice?

That evening, by prearrangement, the campus police ushered me inside Goodell through a back door. There, UMass Student Legal Services attorneys Chuck DiMare and Michele Leaf told me that the administration had just agreed to many of the protesters' demands: to achieve and maintain twenty percent minority undergraduate enrollment; to increase financial aid for those students; to diversify senior administrative and other staff; and to fund new counseling and academic positions that would promote diversity. Not surprisingly, that agreement came with a caveat and a short fuse: the occupiers had to quickly and peacefully leave Goodell.

We lawyers had no doubt that the protesters should take the deal, but when, shortly after my arrival, the one hundred fifty occupiers gathered in the rotunda on the top floor, they began to lambast it. The protesters had made forty-one non-negotiable demands; when they said non-negotiable, they meant non-negotiable; achieving some of them hardly seemed good enough, a woman argued.

An African-American man feared that if the protesters gave up the building, the movement they had ignited would be silenced. A white student angrily asserted that university officials previously had made, and then reneged on, similar promises. Hispanic and Native-American speakers, among others, expressed their belief that without an unequivocal victory, they had a moral duty to go to jail (reminding me of lines from Muriel Rukeyser's poem "Going To Prison:" "The clang of the steel door / It is my choice / But the steel door does clang").

Some complained that their representatives had failed to keep them fully apprised of compromises and decisions made during the negotiations. Others believed that a longer occupation would yield greater success. A few said they felt too tired to think rationally and wanted to go to sleep and talk it over in the morning.

The last position wasn't an option. One way or another, either voluntarily with the settlement in hand or in handcuffs and accompanied by the police, they soon would be leaving Goodell.

DiMare used his introduction to try to cloak me with credibility by informing the students that I had represented many protesters for many years, including anti-nuke demonstrators at the Seabrook nuclear site, union members busted at the Lord Jeffrey Inn in Amherst for a labor protest, and Hampshire College students who had taken over a Northampton State Hospital building the previous year.

After explaining what arrests would entail, I emphasized the significance of the promise of amnesty from both criminal prosecution and university discipline that the UMass administration had proposed as part of the agreement. That amnesty, I argued, would free the protesters to fight for implementation of the accord. Otherwise, they would spend the next few semesters in front of judges presiding in criminal court and administrators conducting disciplinary hearings. And, of course, if they didn't vacate the building, they would have no deal to try to enforce.

After thanking the students for their six days of risk-taking in occupying the building and congratulating them on forcing the university to capitulate on important issues, I argued in favor of accepting the deal—asserting that the best should not become the enemy of the good. After finishing my talk and answering their questions, I felt I had not necessarily convinced anyone of anything.

By 4:30 a.m. there was nothing more for me to say or do. I walked out into a night that was foggy and quiet. Looking back through the windows, I could see the students still debating intensely. I really did not know what they'd decide, or if they would run out of time and the decision would be made for them. As I drove home, the roundtable debate in the rotunda kept resonating, reminding me of discussions at Antioch College more than a quarter century earlier. I felt old.

Frederick Douglass, in his most famous oration, stated, "Power cedes nothing without a demand. It never did, and it never will." Although the principles of the struggle for social justice remain constant, every generation has to learn lessons that cannot be taught, but only learned through experience. Names, faces, places, and demands change, but those differences are nuance.

The next morning the Student Legal Services attorneys telephoned me with the news that the protesters by consensus had accepted the proposal and then held a victory rally outside Goodell. I hadn't slept much, but the news gave me an adrenaline rush and made me feel younger. The students had done well, and they most assuredly had done some good.

April 1997

JEW BOY

'Twas the season. I spent a December afternoon with an attorney general, a district attorney, and a state police investigator consulting about a postcard that had arrived at my office that morning. Addressed to me on Main Street (no building number) in Northampton, it read, "Q. What did Lucerfer (misspelling in original) say after he read the whole Old Testament? A. Thou shall not suffer a Jewboy to live."

"I wanted you to have this," I told the state trooper more dismissively than I felt. "Just in case I end up in a ditch."

My occasional hate mail, usually engendered by a lawsuit I've filed or a position I've publicly espoused as the director of the Western Massachusetts ACLU office, doesn't bother me as much as it first did. Any person who cuts out letters from magazines to construct the words "YOU'LL GET YOURS," signs the epistle "Concerned Citizens," and mails it to me probably is gutless—and harmless—at least in terms of my physical safety. Still, you never know.

Early in my career, a Probate and Family Court judge in Springfield instructed the opposing lawyer and me to come into his chambers. No stenographer was present. I was representing a woman whose husband had deserted her and their four children, divorced her from another state, remarried, and was refusing to pay support. After the judge demanded to know why the case had to go to trial, the other lawyer responded that he had offered me money to settle and then commented, "A smart Jewish lawyer like Mr. Newman should be able to get his client to settle." By resolving the case then, before trial, opposing counsel added as he winked at the judge, I could earn quite a tidy fee with no more work. The two of them—of the same generation, and both with deep roots in Democratic Party politics—shared a laugh over this remark.

Their banter made me cringe, but I feared that if I complained, an unrepentant, indignant judge not only would refuse to recuse himself from the case but also would take out his anger at me on my client. I responded to the judge that when he heard the evidence, he'd appreciate the inadequacy of the offer.

My silence in the face of the lawyer's anti-Semitic comments and the judge's apparent concurrence did not help my client one whit. (Later, confusing the issue further, other, more experienced, lawyers told me they thought the judge was a heartless, misogynist prick, but not an anti-Semite.) The judge loved the military and the ex-husband, who had a full career, twenty years, in the Air Force, and retired as a lieutenant colonel. Throughout the trial, the judge called him "Colonel," did everything but pin a medal on him, and in his decision gave virtually nothing to my client or their kids. Fortunately, the Massachusetts Appeals Court reversed that ruling and, as is customary, remanded the case for a retrial.

We tried the case again in front of the same judge, who once again gave my client the lowest award he thought he could get away with. So we appealed again, and the Appeals Court reversed again.

By the third go-round, the issue had become the amount of attorney's fees the ex-husband would pay me. The judge screwed me yet again, and he was reversed yet again by both the Appeals Court and the Supreme Judicial Court. Finally, the judge, I surmise being tired of the appellate decisions showing him to be—this is the technical legal word—an asshole, recused himself from the case.

At dinner on the day the postcard arrived, I asked my daughters—Jo, age fourteen, and Leah, eleven—their opinion about what the mail had brought. They didn't hesitate. "Do something," they said. "People should know about this."

I shared with them the state police investigator's observation that "Sometimes making a bigger deal just encourages them to do more." Jo and Leah, both unimpressed and undeterred by that position, insisted, "You should do something."

Easier said than done. The police found no fingerprints. The mail brought no further notes. Law enforcement could offer no solution.

Not long after this our kids joined my wife Dale and me watching "In Our Town," a television dramatization of attacks on Jews and other minorities in Billings, Montana, in 1992. Jo asked, "Will those families have to move?" and Leah added, "That couldn't happen here, could it?"

On September 7, 1997, down the road in the liberal town of Amherst, someone smashed the window of Robert Green's typewriter repair store and smeared feces on the wall. After Mr. Green put a sign in his window that said "Why?", white youths repeatedly drove by his store taunting and mocking him, shouting "Why, why." Robert Green is African-American.

Within days, a glass bottle was hurled from a passing car at another African-American man walking along Route 9, and an African-American woman crossing North Pleasant Street in Amherst was accosted with the epithet "nigger bitch." A local landlord served an eviction notice on a Jewish tenant after confiding to a neighbor that he wanted the tenant out "because she was Jewish and only cared about money." And some Amherst College students began distributing the right-wing Liberty Lobby's racist rag, *The Spotlight*, through newspaper boxes placed in front of the college's café and the University of Massachusetts Fine Arts Center.

In response to the vandalism of Mr. Green's store, Amherst residents have organized the Not In Our Town (NIOT) Coalition. The group vows to increase awareness of incidents of racism and bias; offers to bear witness for persons subjected to discrimination because of gender, sexual orientation, religion, race, or disability; and extends advocacy for victims of hate crimes through what NIOT calls a "rapid response network."

We should not be surprised that racist, homophobic, anti-Semitic expression and hate crimes happen in our progressive five college community. They happen everywhere. We share the good fortune that here hatred engenders pushback and outrage.

In 1974, the Warrior Society had taken over an Alexian Brothers novitiate, located just beyond a boundary of the Menominee Indian reservation. This action, a smaller, Wisconsin version of Wounded Knee, resulted in the leaders of the Warrior Society facing serious felony charges, including kidnapping and armed robbery. After law school I moved to the reservation to join the defense team. We called ourselves MLDOC, (pronounced em el doc), The Menominee Legal Defense/Offense Committee.

In the nearby Town of Shawano, you couldn't help but feel the tension between the Indians and the locals. The few whites who, like me, lived on the rez were considered by the townies to be every bit as low, if not lower, than the Indians. Within months of my moving to the rez, a deputy sheriff had shot one of our clients in the back and killed him. In that part of the world, most vehicles were trucks; every truck had a gun rack; and those gun racks held serious rifles. Most people also carried a handgun in a holster or tucked into their waist.

In the fall the cabin that was the home and office of our legal team had been torched. Luckily, no one was in it at the time. The sheriff allegedly had investigated the arson, but no one had been charged. We found another house on the rez, one with a toilet and running water, an upgrade over our previous abode. The state Bureau of Investigation then sent an informant posing as a volunteer to infiltrate our defense team and live with us.

At night on the reservation, there was nothing to do except drink, which I've never done a lot. Thinking it might be fun to play the guitar again, I stopped at the music shop in Shawano, picked out a secondhand one, and asked the fellow working there the price. He responded, "You're not going to try to Jew me down, are you?"

The comment caught me short. I started to say, "What the fuck" but stopped myself. The road from town to the rez often was deserted, and this kid, who somehow knew that's where I was living, struck me as more than capable of shooting out my car tires or windows or at me. I walked out without buying the guitar, but I didn't clearly tell him why. To be sure, when I returned to the rez, my colleagues appreciated my not making more enemies in town, believing we already had more than enough people shooting at us. Still, I considered my response—a non-response really—at best halfbaked.

I hold dear Martin Niemöller's quote: "First they came for the communists, and I didn't speak out because I wasn't a communist; then they came for the socialists, and I didn't speak out because I wasn't a socialist...." and the same for the trade unionists, Jews, and Catholics—with the concluding line, "And when they came for me, there was no one left to speak out."

I said nothing to the guitar-store salesman because I feared I would cause my friends to be hurt or killed, and myself, too. I failed to object when the judge and the lawyer were denigrating Jews because I feared hurting my client. When I first received the postcard with the ostensible death threat, I feared that going after the perpetrator would put my family in danger, but at least this time I pursued the anti-Semite as far as I could.

We can always find reasons to remain silent, and I've found that Niemöller's quote is simpler to recite than to live. Living that integrity and adamancy in the 1960s felt easier because, as Bob Dylan says, "When you ain't got nothing, you got nothing to lose." When you have something, it feels different. Maybe it shouldn't, but it does.

January 1998

NO CLOWNING ALLOWED

On a sunny spring afternoon in western Massachusetts our favorite local clown, JJ Jester, was driving his mini pickup on Rural Route 2, a two-lane road, when a sedan traveling in the opposite lane, trying to pass another car, crossed over the double yellow line on a curve and headed directly toward him. JJ fortunately had quick reactions, and he pulled into the breakdown lane to avoid being killed. A state trooper who witnessed all this didn't go after the vehicular homicidal driver. Rather, having seen the bumper stickers on JJ's truck and caught a glimpse of his hair, a bit grayer but just as wild and long and bushy as it was in the 1960s, pulled him over and then cited him—I'm not making this up—for driving in the breakdown lane. Then the story gets worse.

JJ's truck is plastered with bumper stickers—ones that read "Why Be Normal?" "Question Authority," and "DARE To Think For Yourself," and JJ, of course, looks exactly like the kind of clown who would harbor such thoughts. These sentiments and Mr. Jester's appearance apparently made the state trooper, newly minted from the police academy with a quarter-inch crew cut, feel unkindly toward our clown.

With the party light on top of his cruiser flashing and siren blaring it was easy enough to pull the clown over, but not as simple to figure out what charge would stick. So the trooper went on a treasure hunt in JJ's truck without a warrant or probable cause or reasonable—or even unreasonable—suspicion. Jester, now understanding that this was no laughing matter, considered it wise to watch the cop rummaging around his truck among the fast-food wrappers, tools, and multiple red noses, to see if he would plant anything there.

The trooper then, for reasons he forever would keep a secret, demanded that our merry motorist turn around and not watch him search his truck. But because JJ was a curious—and prudent—clown, he kept peeking at the trooper, who found nothing more interesting than the spare tire. Unfortunately, our clown's curiosity, his constant peeking at the trooper, caused JJ to end up in handcuffs—the kind that don't squirt disappearing ink—and to spend the weekend in the clink. The alleged crime committed for turning and watching? The trooper charged him with disorderly conduct. And don't forget driving in the breakdown lane.

For his trial in rural Orange District Court, our undeterred jester printed up bright orange tickets with a picture of a pointy-nose state trooper going head-to-head with a goofy-looking clown. The ticket gave the bearer a box seat "on the fifty yard line" for a show called "Disorderly Clown."

JJ dressed for court. After all, he had roles to play, the first being a defendant, the second being his own lawyer. Understanding the solemnity of the proceedings, Mr. Jester, for his jury trial, wore a bright orange bow tie that stretched from cheek to cheek and a chartreuse suit. Boring me wore a grey pinstripe for my sidekick role as his ACLU legal advisor.

Halfway through the trial the judge threw out the charges. JJ Jester thereupon donned his size-thirty galoshes, a red nose, and his orange wig, a modest change from his courtroom attire, and on the courthouse steps held a press conference where he proclaimed a victory for clowns everywhere. And also for freedom of speech, which includes bumper stickers. And for the Fourth Amendment right to watch cops while they're conducting unconstitutional searches and seizures.

You might have thought that with this experience, JJ had enough of clowning around with the legal system, but you'd be wrong. The recent presidential campaign sent him back into the political fray. And as you've probably already guessed, where JJ goes, can law enforcement be far behind?

JJ went to Manchester, New Hampshire, to campaign in the first presidential primary. There he donned a six-foot-high phallic costume, used the name Richard Head, and told voters he was running as a write-in candidate for president with the campaign slogan, "He tells the naked truth."

Most people on Manchester's main street thought this was pretty funny stuff. Although a couple cops tried to get someone, anyone, in the crowd to say they were offended, passersby—to the officers' consternation—replied that actually they weren't. Indeed, pedestrians were cheering, and motorists were honking their car horns in appreciation. And JJ, in a prophylactic measure, to insure that no one in fact was offended, told a youngster that he was just a giant mushroom.

Finally, the cops found one woman who, after some prompting, agreed that she disliked Jester's distinctive haberdashery, which allowed the cops to threaten JJ with arrest if he didn't strip it off for—here we go again—disorderly conduct. Jester knew in his heart, having some experience with that charge, that he had not been acting disorderly, so he refused—and yes, JJ, once again—became a busted clown.

At the station, police officers asked JJ to don his homemade phallus again so that they could have Polaroids taken with him. But some humorless, big-brass guy took umbrage at all this and, after the cops delivered him to court, JJ found himself accused not of being disorderly, but rather with being lewd.

This turn of events caused our clown to frown. A lot. In his life, Jester had been called many things. But never lewd.

Fortunately, this clown story, like most, has a happy ending. JJ and the ACLU teamed up again and another judge, noting that the costume was not entirely anatomically accurate, once again threw out the charge.

"I've won the right, proven in a court of law," Jester proclaimed in his victory speech, "for every American, regardless of creed, race, color, age or gender, to put on a penis costume and run for president of the United States...."

Well, not exactly how *Massachusetts Lawyers Weekly* would have put it, but we should leave the last word to Mr. Jester. After all, he really did demonstrate that people who fight to protect freedom of speech come in many guises and when it comes to the First Amendment, JJ has proven himself a stand-up guy.

October 2000

STICK IT

JJ Jester's initial legal travails set me off on a Saturday excursion to downtown Northampton to garner what I knew would be a bumper crop of bumper stickers. Allow me to report the results of my research:

Many bumpers, perhaps to JJ's consternation, endorse DARE—such as "Proud Parent Of A DARE Graduate" and "DARE To Keep Kids Off Drugs." Others, like JJ, dare to express the opposite opinion with slogans like "DARE To Keep Cops Off Donuts"; and "DARE: Donut Abuse Resistance Education." And this one: "HEMP—It's Not Just For Smoking Any More."

Bumper stickers are intended, of course, to communicate—primarily with the folks in the car to the rear, and they often focus on driving: "I'm Only Driving This Way To Piss You Off" and "I Drive As Badly As You Do." My favorite: "Next Time Wave All Your Fingers."

Some parents can't help touting their kids' achievements. "My Son [or Daughter] Is An Honor Student At [insert name of school]." This presumptuousness has engendered the to-the-point response, "My Kid Can Beat Up Your Honor Student."

Guns fire off a lot of car commentary—an occasional NRA advertisement, but more often deadly serious sentiments such as, "If Guns Are Outlawed, Only Outlaws Will Shoot Their Kids Accidentally," and the less pedantic, "I Can't Go To Work Today—The Voices Said To Stay Home And Clean My Guns."

Animal endorsements abound. "I Love My Golden Retriever [Chihuahua, Siamese Cat, Llama]" you name it, a bumper sticker expresses love for it. Animals also engender vegetarian sentiments, such as "Love Animals—Don't Eat Them." With luck, the Subaru sporting that sentiment didn't run into the Pontiac that asserted, "I Love Animals 'Cause They Taste So Good."

The environment also receives attention with declarations such as "Save The Whales" and "Save The Wolves." Occasionally I found "Save The Ales," an ad for local microbreweries. Quite a few admonish us to "Stop Global Warming," and others to "Stop Global Whining."

Here in our liberal, five-college area, cars—not surprisingly—espouse ideas such as "Visualize World Peace," which has spawned spin-offs including, "Visualize Whirled Peas" and "Visualize Grilled Cheese" as well as the expected, "Friends Don't Let Friends Vote Republican." These sentiments are offset by a large number, mostly on trucks, that read "Annoy A Liberal. Work Hard And Be Happy." Generally though, the thoughts convey an unaggressive approach to the world: "Guano Happens," even one or two "Grace Happens."

Politicians in general and Congress in particular apparently provide easy targets: "Politicians And Diapers Need To Be Changed Often—For The Same Reason," "If Progress Means To Move Forward, What Does Congress Mean?" and "Invest In America: Buy A Congressman."

Because we are, after all, talking about Northampton, feminist sentiments cover the roads: "Feminism Is The Radical Notion That Women Are People"; "Ginger Rogers Did Everything Fred Astaire Did, Only Backwards And In High Heels"; "I Believe In Dragons, Good Men And Other Fantasy Creatures." Also, "How Many Roads Must A Man Go Down Before He Admits He Is Lost." Top prize in this category: "Grow Your Own Dope—Plant A Man."

Because I work for the ACLU, I felt compelled to award my personal grand prize to the one that revised Voltaire's aphorism to say, "I May Not Agree With Your Bumper Sticker, But I'll Defend Your Right To Stick It."

March 1999

BUNNY KING

"Her lesbian household," a Greenfield, Massachusetts, Family Court judge wrote in Bunny King's case, decided in 1979, *"creates an element of instability that would adversely affect the welfare of the children. [Therefore], she will [only] be allowed to visit with her daughters two (2) hours each week under the supervision of the Probation officer...."*

Bunny King had lived a hardscrabble life—a lousy marriage, little money, and bouts with serious medical conditions, including potentially fatal deep thrombophlebitis that required multiple hospitalizations and long recuperation periods. During those times when she was physically unable to care for her two young daughters, Bunny entrusted their care to her friend Magdalena. At one point she arranged for Magdalena to be officially appointed their guardian so that Magdalena could authorize medical treatments for the kids and talk to their teachers.

While the kids were living with her, Magdalena converted to fundamentalist Christianity, which forbade homosexuality, and after Bunny, who was a lesbian, recuperated and asked for her kids back, Magdalena said no.

Lawsuits regarding custody were filed, but they languished in the courts—nothing happened. Then, one day when she was visiting with her kids, Bunny failed to return them to Magdalena and absconded with them to Vermont. There, the kids thrived, but after some months the Vermont police arrested Bunny for kidnapping. The police officer who handcuffed Bunny would later testify at trial that the children told him that they loved their mother and didn't want to go back to live with Magdalena. The state returned them to Magdalena anyway.

Not long after the kidnapping charges were dismissed, my law partner Wendy Sibbison and I were retained to represent Bunny.

At the time of her trial in late 1978, an openly gay parent fighting for custody made front page news in the local paper, *The Recorder*, and in the regional paper of record, *The Republican*, as well. One morning, with *The Recorder*'s reporter elsewhere in the courthouse but with *The Republican*'s ensconced in our courtroom, a witness testified to the name and occupation of Bunny's life partner.

That snippet of testimony caused Wendy Sibbison and me to rush over to *The Republican*'s office during the lunch break to plead with Ralph Gordon, the reporter and bureau chief, to not include the name of Bunny's partner in his next day's story. Bunny's partner taught high school and if the school system found out she was gay, we had little doubt that she would be fired. Ralph was a crusty, tough, old-school, just-tell-me-the-facts reporter. After an hour of our arguing, cajoling and importuning, he turned us down.

Wendy and I left the newspaper office feeling horrible. Not only, it seemed, could this trial very well end up with Bunny not getting her kids back, but in the process we might cost her partner the job she loved.

Reading *The Republican* the next morning, we found that Ralph had not included Bunny's partner's name or occupation in his story. We felt relief and gratitude, celebrated in the hallway outside the courtroom for a minute or two, and then walked back in to the tension of the trial, which lasted three more days. The judge then took four weeks to write his decision, which said we lost. He pointed to *"her lesbian household creat[ing]...an element of instability..."* as a primary reason.

We waited almost a year for the Massachusetts Supreme Judicial Court to schedule the oral argument on our appeal and another three months after the argument for the court to issue its decision. The opinion from the state's highest court, when it finally came, contained these welcome words: "The State may not deprive parents of custody of their children simply because [they] embrace ideologies or lifestyles at odds with the average...." Bunny's sexual preference, the court ruled, was "irrelevant to consideration of parental skills...."

Today, the truth of that judicial declaration seems obvious. In 1980 in this—the first—gay custody case to be decided by any state's highest court, it wasn't at all.

The Supreme Judicial Court's ruling sent the case back to the Franklin County Family Court to see if all things—except her sexual preference—considered, it was in the children's best interest to live with their mom. After another trial, the same judge who had denied Bunny custody because she was a lesbian returned her daughters to her.

Although Bunny's case was important both politically and as precedent, she did not consider herself a particularly political person. She would not have chosen to champion a cause. She just wanted to mother her daughters and live with her life partner.

Former Speaker of the U.S. House of Representatives Tip O'Neal famously stated that all politics are local. Similarly, all civil rights cases are local. They start with one person who is compelled and willing to fight for her rights and what is right. Bunny did that. She won for herself, and she won for all the families whose cases came after hers.

Recently, after hearing of Bunny's death, I called her partner, Linda Allen. Linda told me that she remembered vividly that anxiety-filled day over seventeen years ago, waiting for the newspapers to be delivered to the newsstand. She also told me that she still teaches at the same school.

Linda reminisced that Bunny, an open and honest person, would have wanted what was said about her at the close of her life to be open and honest. That's what her daughters wanted, too. After she died in December 1995, Linda and Bunny's daughters provided the information for Bunny's obituary in the local newspapers, which read:

"Bunny Anne King, 42, died Tuesday (12/19/95) ... [S]he devoted her time to Bunny King's Kreations, creating a variety of craft items ....She was a Girl Scout leader for Troops 94 and 494 in Shelburne Falls from 1981 to 1992 .... Besides her parents ... she leaves two daughters, four sisters ... a grandson ... and her partner of twenty years ... Linda M. Allen of Shelburne Falls ...."

January 1996

DORIUS AND SPOFFORD

In April 1961, the question before the trustees of all-women Smith College was whether professors Ned Spofford and Joel Dorius, being gay, were morally fit to teach there. The trustees considered the question, answered, emphatically, "No," and fired them.

Now forty years later, *"The Scarlet Professor: Newton Arvin, A Literary Life Shattered by Scandal,"* by Northampton author Barry Werth, is shining a national and local spotlight on the current trustees as they consider whether or not to renounce and ameliorate their predecessors' homophobia-motivated firings. Next month the trustees once again will decide how to treat Dorius and Spofford.

The Scarlet Professor describes how in 1960 the comfortable academic life of Newton Arvin, a Smith College professor of literature and a famous literary critic, came crashing down around him when the Massachusetts State Police Vice Squad arrested him on pornography charges. Arvin panicked and named names. He gave up Smith junior professors Dorius and Spofford as fellow homosexuals and possessors of similar pornography—mostly muscleman magazines, laughably mild by today's standards.

After his arrest, Arvin, who had taught at Smith since 1924, with a long and distinguished academic career behind him, retired. But Dorius and Spofford, gifted teachers and scholars but also young and untenured, wanted to remain at Smith.

And if the opinion of the faculty, students, and administrators had mattered, they would have. The faculty voted overwhelmingly for Dorius and Spofford to retain their positions. The student newspaper, *The Sophian,* supported them. Smith's president, Thomas Mendenhall, believed they deserved to continue to teach at the college. And the Massachusetts

Supreme Judicial Court eventually would throw out the possession of pornography charges lodged against them.

But the majority of the Board of Trustees, all white, male, and rich, held beliefs that reflected the ideology of their class and gender. As reported in *The Scarlet Professor*, they could easily accept, if not condone, the affairs that male professors often had with their students, but in contrast they believed that homosexuals, "were ultimately weak, abominable, predatory creatures.... Like communists, they preyed on America's youth and were unreliable. Smith was a liberal institution, but this was no time to indulge liberal sympathies," so they fired them. According to Spofford, his termination by Smith caused him to suffer a series of mental breakdowns and hospitalizations, and Dorius, too, has suffered for four decades.

Werth's book has exposed a chapter of Smith's history that the college—almost miraculously from a public relations standpoint—had successfully shoved down a memory hole. In the 1960s, by design, the college made no mention of them, and as the years passed, no one remembered them either. Werth's book has changed that.

In 1961, the story of the arrest of Newton Arvin, a leading academic, was featured in *The New York Times, The Boston Globe,* and newspapers across America. In 2001 the national media once again has been telling the story. Locally, *The Scarlet Professor* has caused the Northampton Human Rights Commission to call upon Smith College and its trustees to offer Spofford and Dorius "appropriate and adequate compensation" and to apologize to them.

How hard could that be?

Smith College's endowment of approximately $1 billion yields over a million dollars of income each week. In addition, the college, in the midst of a $425 million capital campaign, is raising an additional $100 million each year. Smith can afford to spend almost any amount it wants on whatever it wants. For the college, not paying a bill is a matter of choice.

What amount of money would do justice for ruined reputations, damaged lives, forfeited careers, and the emotional havoc the trustees caused? No one can know for sure, but here's a suggestion: compensate them both $25,000 per year for 40 years or $1 million and, in addition, establish The Joel Dorius and Ned Spofford Chair for Gay and Lesbian Studies.

For the first century of its existence, Smith, although a college for women only, had only male presidents. Nellie Mendenhall, the wife of Smith President Thomas Mendenhall, recalled that after the ignominious meeting at which they fired Dorius and Spofford, "several of the Trustees returned to the mansion [the president's house] for their suitcases.... As they departed the front hall one of them [said], 'I'll see you at vespers this afternoon.' They had just crucified two guys and were going off to celebrate the crucifixion of another."

In 1961, the question before the trustees was, What is the ethical, moral and honest decision to make regarding Professor Dorius and Professor Spofford? Four decades later the question remains the same.

September 2001

So what did the trustees do in October 2001, when they were given the opportunity to remedy forty years of injustice?

They met, they talked, they consumed sumptuous meals, and at the end decided to kick the can down the road and postpone any decision until their next meeting in April, 2002. And at that April meeting, what did they do?

The trustees decided to offer Dorius and Spofford—get this—nothing—not even an apology. Rather, they voted to affirm the college's nondiscrimination policy and allocate up to $100,000 (a sum that equals about ten hours of interest on the college's endowment) to fund a one-time set of lectures and a symposium on various civil liberties topics. The Smith press release that followed the trustees' decision failed to mention that Dorius and Spofford had been fired or why, and it did not contain the word "gay" or "homosexual," thus resurrecting the public relations approach that had worked so well for the college for four decades.

Smith fancies itself almost as prestigious as Harvard, which has been described as an investment firm with a university attached. Smith resembles Harvard in that regard. Like large corporations, it zealously protects its brand, pays lawyers and investment advisors millions, and exploits people when it finds it expedient to do so. My years representing the union of housekeepers and food service workers—mostly women—at Smith has taught me that.

In response to the trustees' condonation of their predecessors' bigotry, the chair of the city's Human Rights Commission, Marjorie Hess, said, "It is not enough." Werth concurred, commenting that the trustees' inaction "reminded [him] of the Peggy Lee song, 'Is That All There Is?'" The regional newspaper, *The Republican*, in an extremely rare editorial critical of Smith, wrote that "Dorius and Spofford were victims of a witch hunt .... The college needs to apologize [because] lectures [about] civility and academic freedom will ring hollow until it does."

Chimes from Smith College's four sets of bells in various college buildings, including the one with forty-eight bells in the carillon in College Hall, often can be heard throughout the campus. Unbeknownst to the Smith community, they have rung hollow for the past forty years. Apparently the trustees don't much care if they ring hollow for the next forty as well.

April 2002

Addendum

About a month after the trustees' decision, Lani Guinier, a hero of the civil rights movement and the first African-American tenured professor at Harvard Law School, delivered a moving commencement address at Smith. At that ceremony the college also presented honorary degrees to two other heroes of our time, Professor Anita Hill, author of *Speaking Truth to Power*, the story of her testimony at the Clarence Thomas confirmation hearings, and Katha Pollitt, *The Nation* magazine's acclaimed progressive columnist. It's inconceivable that these women—if they had known—would have condoned what the college had done, yet again, to Dorius and Spofford. But the timing of the trustees actions—with final exams and graduation approaching—prevented the students from effectively organizing and challenging that decision.

The timing was intentional. The trustees appreciated that if the story of Dorius and Spofford spread across the campus, the students would have organized and protested, perhaps loudly and forcefully enough to compel the trustees to change their decision.

Smith College students have proven themselves enormously effective political organizers and leaders, both practical and idealistic. In contract talks with the college on behalf of its housekeepers and food service workers, students have joined the union negotiation team, led communication efforts, protested at graduation, and challenged the administration to treat decently and pay fairly these low wage earners—mostly women employees—who clean the dorms and cook the food. Because of their efforts, Smith has been forced to be less cheap and more fair.

Smith's trustees apparently still have no compunctions about *The Boston Globe* editorial, written in 1981 in response to the housekeepers' and food service workers' fight for a decent pension, titled "Women and Mammon at Smith." Fortunately, Smith students refuse to acquiesce to the class bias of the trustees and their administrators.

ROBBY'S PARENTS

Robby Meeropol and I were talking about the events immediately preceding his parents' execution in the electric chair at the infamous upstate New York maximum security prison, Sing Sing, in 1953. The reason for the conversation?

The National Security Agency recently has released summaries of encrypted 1945 Soviet diplomatic radio messages about his parents, Julius and Ethel Rosenberg. The government's press release accompanying those summaries claimed that the documents demonstrate that Julius and Ethel had spied for the Soviet Union and committed espionage against the United States. The mainstream media has uncritically regurgitated that assertion. The real story is more dramatic.

The documents on the desk in front of us had a black line through the "Top Secret" stamp on each page. Those papers demonstrate that Robby's father Julius, who was a Communist, spied for the Soviet Union during World War II and that he provided industrial secrets when Russia was our ally, but not that he ever stole any atomic secrets when the Soviet Union was our Cold War enemy.

What secrets Julius stole, and when he stole them, matters. Robby's (and his brother Michael's) parents were executed for providing "the secret of the atomic bomb" to the Soviet Union. If Julius didn't do that, even the government agrees, his parents should not have been sent to the electric chair.

In 1973, more than twenty years after their trial, the government made public the drawings of "the secret of the atomic bomb" that the Rosenbergs allegedly helped to divulge to the U.S.S.R. Atomic scientists described those diagrams as "baby drawings," "crude," and "useless," containing "ludicrously little" information. The alleged secret for which they ostensibly were executed turns out to be high school–level information that even in the 1950s had been available at any public library.

Robby pointed out other parts of these newly declassified documents. The major reference to his mother, Ethel, says, "Knows about her husband's work. In view of delicate health does not work. Is characterized positively as a devoted person." In the encrypted Soviet messages Ethel doesn't even have an alias. Because she never joined any spy ring and never acted as their agent, the Soviets had no reason to give her one.

A month before the Rosenberg trial was scheduled to begin, in February 1951, at a secret meeting of the Joint Congressional Committee on Atomic Energy, government prosecutors admitted that they had virtually no evidence against Ethel. But, testified a prosecutor, "If we can convict [Ethel], too, and get a stiff sentence of twenty-five to thirty years, that may serve to make this fellow [Julius] disgorge." The government wanted Julius to name names, specifically the names of other communists and fellow travelers.

But the government faced a seemingly insurmountable obstacle in the case against Ethel. The two main witnesses—Ethel's brother, David Greenglass, and his wife, Ruth, both independently had informed the Federal Bureau of Investigation (FBI) many times that Ethel Rosenberg had never participated in their spy ring. In order to convict Ethel, that lacuna in the evidence needed to be filled. As the prosecutors well understood, a few simple lies would suffice. After all, the Rosenbergs were charged with conspiracy to commit espionage, not actually committing it. Conspiracy fundamentally requires only proof of an agreement, proof that can be inferred.

Ten days before trial, Ruth Greenglass, according to the FBI, suddenly remembered that Ethel had typed Julius's notes about atomic material. Two days later, according to the FBI, David Greenglass provided corroboration, recalling that his wife Ruth had informed him that Julius had told her that Ethel had typed the notes. Then, on the eve of the trial, David Greenglass, contrary to his previous statements to the FBI, substituted the name Ethel Rosenberg for his wife Ruth as the person who had recruited him into the spy ring. In the anti-Communist hysteria of 1951, the Greenglasses' perjury, bolstered by the truth that Ethel was a Communist married to another Communist, gave the government more than evidence enough to convict her.

Prosecutors knew Ethel was innocent of the charge. Indeed, in July 1953, as the execution date approached, the FBI offered her this deal: if you confess that your husband Julius stole atomic secrets for the Soviet Union, we won't electrocute you. The FBI believed its "talk or die" offer would compel the Rosenbergs to recant their denials. In anticipation, the agency composed questions for Julius. So convinced was the bureau of Ethel's lack of involvement that it didn't even bother to write any questions for her. The sixth question to Julius read, "Was your wife cognizant of your activities?"

In her clemency petition to President Eisenhower, Ethel wrote, "We are innocent.... To forsake this truth is to pay too high a price even for the priceless gift of life.... We are not martyrs.... We do not want to die .... We long to see our two sons...."

On July 18, 1950, Supreme Court Justice William O. Douglas stayed the execution. Apparently tried under the wrong law, the justice ruled that the Rosenbergs could not legally be candidates for capital punishment. But, on July 19, Chief Justice Fred Vinson, having secretly promised Attorney General Herbert Brownell that the Rosenbergs would die as scheduled, summoned the full court back into emergency session to reverse Douglas's decision. At eight o'clock that evening the government strapped the Rosenbergs into the electric chair, first Julius, then Ethel.

No court has ever resolved the merits of the extraordinary error of the Rosenbergs being tried and put to death for a crime for which they were not charged. Justice Felix Frankfurter, in his opinion published after the execution, said, "Writing ... [about] two lives after the curtain has ... wrung down ... has the appearance of pathetic futility. But history also has its claims."

In her last letter to her sons, Ethel wrote, "Know that life is worth the living.... We [are] comforted in the sure knowledge that others will carry on after us."

From 1988 through 1989, Robby met regularly with us defense lawyers for the Ohio 7, seven political radicals charged with seditious conspiracy—a conspiracy to overthrow the United States government by force or violence. Pre-trial hearings and jury selection in that case consumed over six months. Some of those hearings focused on the FBI agents' misconduct after they arrested our clients and seized their children.

Our motions called upon the federal judge to penalize the government for holding the kids incommunicado for several weeks, repeatedly interrogating eleven- and nine-year-olds without any adult other than SWAT team members present, at times threatening them, at other times trying to bribe them with money and Big Macs. The judge listened attentively to the evidence and then imposed no sanctions on the government.

After that decision, there still remained unanswered the more significant legal question raised by the indictment—the guilt or innocence of our clients.

Forget the absurdity of the idea that seven people, including three couples with kids, could overthrow the government of the United States. Remember, they weren't charged with sedition—but rather with a conspiracy to commit sedition. All the government had to prove was an agreement that they wanted to do that. Hell, in the 1960s we all wanted to do that "So what's the crime?" many left-leaning political activists in our community asked.

The indictment of The Ohio 7 reminded us that the government could indict almost any political opponent. The defense committee had tee shirts silk-screened with the slogan "Join The Conspiracy." Ironic, and sometimes gallows, humor helped sustain the defense lawyers. Goodness knows we needed sustaining. The government intended to imprison our clients for decades—or for life.

After a trial that lasted more than eleven months the jury rendered its verdict: not guilty. That afternoon some of us on the defense team went for a run around the reservoir in nearby Holyoke. Adrenaline made me run faster than I ever have before, and I wore a tee shirt with the slogan "Miracles Happen."

That case, and the government's treatment of our clients' children, inspired Robby to found the Rosenberg Fund for Children. The RFC provides for the educational and emotional needs of children whose parents have been targeted because of their political beliefs and progressive activism. I've served on the board of directors since its inception.

As Robby and I were talking, I jotted down some notes about the recent revelations about his parents on RFC stationery. The stationery bears the organization's motto, "Carry it forward. Pass it on."

August 1995

BIG BLACK

I met Frank "Big Black" Smith in 1987 because the New York lawyers on our "Ohio 7" seditious conspiracy defense team thought that Black, as they called him, was the best investigator and paralegal they knew. They wanted him on the case with us.

Black then was 54 years old, 6' 2" tall, and 280 pounds, with a weight lifter's arms, a quick, big smile, and a voice and a laugh that could fill a ballroom. You could see why witnesses would willingly talk to him. Mostly it was the grip of his handshake and his smile when he said hello.

Over the next few days I learned that Big Black had been locked up in Attica State Prison for over six years, serving a fifteen-year sentence for robbing a street crap game, when the uprising occurred there in 1971. Attica erupted, most penologists agree, because convicts, too long treated like animals, had been pushed beyond their breaking point.

As *The New York Times* reported, after the guards retook the prison, they forced Black to lie naked for four to six hours on a picnic table, stuck a football under his chin, and threatened to first castrate and then kill him if the football squirmed loose. As he lay there, the guards dropped lighted cigarettes and hot shotgun shells on his stomach and smacked his testicles with their nightsticks. Later they made him walk barefoot over broken glass through a gauntlet of guards who beat him with their batons and rifle butts.

Sixteen years later, in 1997, Big Black finally had his trial against the prison officials. He won. The truth finally had come out. There was no justification for the attack on the inmates. The state had committed atrocities and murder. All this from a conservative, upstate New York jury.

Black was represented by attorney Elizabeth Fink, who has been representing the Attica inmates and their families for over a quarter of a century and was leading the charge for the defense in our seditious conspiracy case as well. Black was the first of 1281 Attica plaintiff inmates to have his case heard.

Black was lucky. He survived prison. After his release in 1973, he found a profession, a calling. He married and has three children and five grandchildren. His story, that of an ex-con who succeeded on the outside despite years of being caged inside the razor wire, provides a testament to human resiliency. Few fare as well.

In *A Time to Die*, about the Attica uprising, Tom Wicker writes that we tolerate conditions in American prisons that go far beyond punishment—what we today would call torture—in part because we never hear or read about them. The walls and the razor wire, he points out, are designed more to keep outsiders out than to keep prisoners in. As for who bears responsibility, "All society was the keeper of the caged," Wicker writes. "At Attica the men with the clubs were only its agents."

July 1997

OUR IRISH ROOTS

Heather was beaming. Having glimpsed our thirteen-year-old daughter Leah's red hair, misheard my last name as Noonan, and learned that we had landed in Shannon Airport that morning on our first trip to Ireland, she enthusiastically congratulated us in her thick Irish brogue, "So you've come to find your roots, have ya?"

Some forty-four million Americans claim Irish ancestry, and many have taken pilgrimages to Ireland to find their families' villages, homes, parishes, or graves. Heather, our bed-and-breakfast host, assumed that we had begun a similar journey.

And she looked so bubbly about our finding our roots that I felt bad telling her that we had no connection to Castlegregory, Cork, or Killarney. "I'm afraid not," I replied. "We're Eastern European Jewish stock."

Her smile faded, but she would not be deterred easily. "Well, perhaps your people have a bit of Irish. Americans are so mixed, you know."

But I can claim no Irish familial history. Although 1800 Jews live in Dublin, which has three synagogues and one Kosher butcher, and, in the 1950s, had a Jewish lord mayor, Robert Briscoe, in general Jews do not unearth their legacies in Ireland. My ancestors emigrated to the United States in the mid-1800s—on my father's side from Austria-Hungary and Germany; on my mother's from Russia. My paternal great-great-grandfather arrived with a set of clothes, a watch, and the equivalent of fifteen cents. My maternal great-great-grandparents had about the same.

I considered, but resisted, telling Heather that I have relatives on my mother's side named Burke. Burke, often a fine Irish surname to be sure, also derives from Jewish names such as Burkowitz that, like many names, Ellis Island customs agents refused to write down.

The alteration of surnames, however, would pose a comparatively tiny obstacle in any search for my family's pre-emigration roots. In Russia, Germany, and Austria the synagogues long ago were razed, the street signs destroyed, the graves desecrated, and the records burned. Any remnants of heritage that might have survived the pogroms were consumed during the world wars and the Third Reich.

"Sorry," I said to Heather, "I don't think we'll find roots here."

But I read a lot of history on our trip and, before leaving Ireland, realized that what I had said to Heather was wrong.

Between 1169 and 1845 the English subjugated this island nation numerous times. Even after the 1801 Act of Union joined Ireland to Great Britain, English governance of Ireland effectively constituted a military occupation.

The Irish Penal Laws, instituted in 1695 and not repealed until 1830, proscribed practicing Catholicism; barred Catholics from every civic activity, including attending school; prohibited Catholics from owning land; and treated priest-hunting as sport. Edmund Burke, the eighteenth-century Irish-born British politician and writer, described these laws as "a machine as well fitted for the oppression, impoverishment and degradation of a people...as ever proceeded from the perverted ingenuity of man."

In Cecil Woodham-Smith's *The Great Hunger: Ireland, 1845–1849*, the story of the potato famine of the 1840s which killed one million Irish peasants, one passage describes a paradigm of England's treatment of the Irish. It was in 1847 that "the Tralee Council sent a piteous memorial: the district was starving...and they implored the government to act...the government responded [only] by sending additional troops...."

Ireland's population, decimated by death, was also dramatically reduced by the loss of three million emigrants escaping starvation and disease. Many fled to the United States on vermin-filled vessels the Irish called "coffin ships." Those immigrants who survived the passage eventually flourished in America—despite anti-Irish, anti-Catholic bias. Those who stayed fought for and, with Great Britain's tacit approval in 1920, won independence for most of Ireland.

Jews have a similar story. Six million were exterminated during the Holocaust. Then in 1948 the state of Israel, again with British acquiescence, seized its independence. And in America, despite anti-Semitism, Jews, too, have flourished.

In Ireland I realized that I needed no blood ancestry there to understand that the Jews and the Irish, like so many others, share a common taproot of humanity: they have suffered, endured, and overcome. Unfortunately the lessons those victories have taught must be constantly relearned. The recent Irish Republican Army bombing of a hospital in Dublin and Israel's continued quarantining of Palestinians dramatically illustrate how political expediency, combined with historical anger, can destroy common decency and our common humanity.

Ireland's Nobel Prize–winning poet William Butler Yeats warned against such vengeance: "A beggar upon horseback lashes a beggar upon foot,/ Hurrah for revolution.... / The beggars have changed places but the lash goes on." Similarly, the Israeli historian Yehuda Bauer has written that the Holocaust teaches, "Thou shalt not be a victim. Thou shalt not be a perpetrator." From these initial lessons grows another: "Above all, thou shalt not be a bystander."

To these essential roots we all are connected. Through them we are all sustained.

November 1996

MARIONIZING MASSACHUSETTS

Prisons sleep. I learned this on my first visit to a maximum security penitentiary, Massachusetts Correctional Institution (MCI) at Walpole, as a law student, in 1972.

After the riots there that year, I volunteered as a civilian observer and was assigned to the graveyard shift. We civilians walked the catwalks on the tiers and tried not to invade the privacy of the men in the cages. We would glance at those forms under their coarse blankets, but then quickly shift our eyes and stare mostly at the walls across from the windowless cells. Those walls, sixty feet high and ten feet thick, were slopped with a frieze of food and human feces.

By three or four in the morning, dream-noises and the cicada sound of beds creaking from masturbating or shifting bodies would now and then disturb the night. Mostly it was quiet.

By seven, however, the volume was cranking up: a non-stop cacophony of arguing or jiving or just mindless mouthing off for want of anything else to do; banging and hollering and hooting, one inmate louder than the next, competing by the unwritten rule that he who screams the loudest wins the argument and makes it to the next moment feeling victorious over someone, about something. In Walpole then—as in most prisons—the incessant noise, with only minor lulls, would ratchet up all day until the count was conducted, all the men were shut back into their cells, lights dimmed, the noise at long last would subside, and the institution again slept.

Prisoners who know how to do time understand the importance of capturing sleep. Between the time guards shut off the lights and turn them on again, some 28,000 seconds go by. A sleepless night can mean counting every one or lying in the dark with thoughts pinging in your head like loose coins in a dryer.

Sometimes something amorphous and unidentified steals the night's sleep. More often, concrete bad news makes the prisoner count those 28,000 seconds: an appeal lost, a visit missed, a parole application denied; or an inmate twice your size promising to soap up your anus and rape you during your next shower.

In his book *In Constant Fear*, Peter Remick, doing time at Walpole for armed robbery, wrote: "The majority of the inmates want a safe institution where they can sleep without fear of someone knifing them to death. They want to walk the prison corridor without fear of being beaten on the head with lead pipes and steel bars. They want to know that other inmates won't pull knives and demand their canteen tickets, radios, and TVs or attack them sexually."

Fear of HIV infection, of course, compounds the fear of sexual attacks. Male prisoners commit over 200,000 rapes on other male prisoners every year. Some guards also sexually abuse and rape prisoners. Seven percent of Massachusetts inmates are HIV positive.

Here's the most outrageous part: generally we are not locking up dangerous people. Only fifteen percent of federal and 32 percent of state inmates are incarcerated for violent crimes. Prisons are bulging with persons sentenced for nonviolent drug and property offenses.

The imprisoned, overwhelmingly, are poor (33 percent were unemployed prior to entering jail) and, disproportionately, people of color. More African-American men are incarcerated than are enrolled in colleges and universities. About fifty percent of the prison population is black, and nearly eight percent is Hispanic.

Richard Nixon declared a war on crime during his 1972 presidential campaign. That war has been waged like the war in Vietnam War—with body counts as the standard for success.

By that criterion, as in Vietnam, we have won. In 1972 Americans were incarcerating 200,000 of our own; by 1984, 400,000; by 1991, 1,000,000; and by 1994, 1,500,000. By the year 2000, our prison population is expected to exceed 2,000,000. An additional 4,000,000 are on probation or parole—for a total of 5,500,000 Americans enmeshed in the criminal justice system at any one time.

With an incarceration rate between five and eight times that of Canada and Western European countries, the United States today locks up a greater percentage of its population than any other nation in the world. And every week the United States puts 1524 new prison cells on line and locks 2000 more people behind bars.

We warehouse millions of nonviolent, rehabilitatable individuals in institutions where they are brutalized both psychologically and physically and then release them jobless, skill-less, uneducated, and broke. We have disconnected them from their families and their communities, left their mental health problems and substance abuse untreated, and burdened them with the stigma of being ex-cons. The released, not surprisingly, commit more crimes. As demonstrated by the grates on apartment windows, triple deadbolt locks on front doors, walled communities, and the proliferation of alarms on almost everything, our policy of senselessly imprisoning others results mostly in imprisoning ourselves.

And at great expense: it costs between $50,000 and $100,000 to build a cell and almost $30,000 per year to imprison an inmate in one.

When I began practicing law in 1976, the sentencing hearing that would determine the months, years, and possibly decades my client would serve behind bars—if he served time at all—constituted a crucial part of my and any competent criminal defense lawyer's practice. In any serious case we would secure affidavits, therapist reports, evaluations and prognoses, and recommendations from family, friends, employers, landlords and coworkers, as well as army discharge papers, and records from schools, hospitals, half-way houses, and foster homes—anything that would help humanize the client. We'd cite these testimonials as well as journals and medical treatises to help explain why he or she committed the crime. We'd write a memorandum to demonstrate how a carefully crafted sentence, involving minimal or no incarceration, could rehabilitate Mr. Jones or Ms. Smith and lead to a productive life while at the same time ensuring public safety.

If we actually had nothing substantive to say—a rare case indeed—we could always write and argue about everything Mr. Jones or Ms. Smith was denied as a child and as an adult as well, or describe the sexual or other abuse our client suffered while in foster care or married, or highlight a dysfunctional birth family and plead for the court to give him or her the chance that the client had always been denied.

Whenever possible we'd bring witnesses to the sentencing hearing—mom, dad, wife, kids. We'd have the adults testify. Many judges, certainly not all, cannot as easily dispense years in prison as if they were M&Ms when the defendant, whose name the judge can recall only by repeatedly glancing at the papers on his bench, becomes an actual person who could live a good life if the judge, through his sentence, doesn't destroy it. The district attorney would respond in myriad ways, all of which asserted, more or less, that vengeance and punishment equate with justice.

The system, of course, recognizes punishment as one, but only one, of the legitimate objectives of sentencing. Rehabilitation also plays a part, as do considerations of specific deterrence (imposing a sanction that diminishes the possibility of that defendant committing another crime); incapacitation (protecting society while the offender is incarcerated); and general deterrence (setting an example that will stop others from similar criminal behavior). After weighing these factors, the theory goes, a judge will craft an appropriate sentence. A good sentencing hearing, prepared and conducted by a dedicated defense lawyer, could make a difference.

A client of mine—who other lawyers, the district attorney and the probation officer all assumed would be sentenced to direct time for her part in an armed robbery but wasn't (she was put on probation)—sent me one of those faux newspapers with this headline: "Atty. Bill Newman Did For Me What F. Lee Bailey Couldn't Do For Patty Hearst." I framed it. Every time I see it, I feel proud. By the way, twenty years have gone by, and she has never been in any trouble with the law again.

The result in that case couldn't happen today. Today that client would serve at least a decade, and more likely two. Mandatory minimums and sentencing guidelines have transmogrified judges from ostensibly learned people with some wisdom, who dispense justice, into funtionaries with adding machines. These sentencing laws also mean that the D.A. or U.S. Attorney, by dint of his authority to select the crime to charge, as a practical matter, is empowered to sentence the defendant as well.

More people in prison serving longer sentences, and the obvious consequence—a larger prison population—required Massachusetts to construct a new penological model. Prison officials found that paradigm in the United States Penitentiary-Marion, a federal prison in Illinois that in 1984 was ordered placed in permanent "lockdown." Marion at the time constituted a large-scale experiment in sensory deprivation but now no longer is an experiment, but rather a norm.

Under Marion's model, prisoners are confined to their cells not less than twenty-three hours a day. Authorities allow prisoners out three times a week for "exercise." Arms shackled and legs chained, an inmate shuffles from his cell into a cage on wheels, just big enough for a man to fit inside. A guard rolls that cage into another, larger one. All the prisoner can do is walk—eight or ten steps in one direction—eight or ten steps back. Prisoners appropriately call the cage the "run," or the "pound." So do the guards.

But the guards don't talk to the prisoners, and the prisoners, sealed behind triple-plated steel doors, can't talk to each other. They also cannot see outside their cells. Meals on trays are slid into their individual cages through what looks like a mail slot.

In 1994 Marion moved lock, stock, and barrel to Florence, Colorado. Like Marion, Florence magnifies an eerie quiet. From time to time, from one of the 1400 iron doors opening and closing, a metallic sound echoes, but in this above-ground mausoleum you can rarely hear another sound.

Except, of course, for the screaming in individual cells. Evidence in the lawsuit filed on account of the lockdown showed that guards would shackle prisoners in their cells and kick them with steel-tipped boots and beat them with three-foot riot bludgeons. According to the guards, sometimes they would also conduct rectal searches that amounted to rape and other times shove their riot batons up inmates' rectums. Guards also would use, on shackled inmates, rib spreaders—equipment that separates rib cartilage and inflicts searing pain, but breaks no bones and leaves no evidence of bruising. The prison distributes these rib spreaders to guards as part of regular-issue equipment.

According to federal officials, beatings are in the eye of the beholder. The assistant warden opined under oath that a prisoner was not "beaten" unless the prison hospitalized him in an intensive care unit. A kick to the stomach of a handcuffed prisoner did not amount to "abuse or beating."

In a ruling on the prisoners' claims, the federal appeals court first recited the facts:

> *Inmates are forbidden to socialize with each other or to participate in group religious services. Inmates who ... misbehave ... are sometimes tied spread-eagle on their beds, often for hours at a stretch. Inmates returning to their cells are subject[ed] to a rectal search [even though the inmate has not been in contact with any other human being, because visits are conducted by monitored telephones through thick glass]. A paramedic inserts a gloved finger into the inmate's rectum and feels around for a knife or other weapon or contraband....*

The Court then articulated part of the inmates' legal claims:

> *The [prisoners] argue that the conditions ... are even worse than depicted above because guards frequently beat prisoners and conduct the rectal searches in an unnecessarily brutal, painful and humiliating manner....These allegations [and others] aroused the [condemnation] of Amnesty International.*

Then came the "but." The appellate court, after reciting the constitutional mantra—that prisons must reflect "society's evolving standards of decency"—held that Marion was close enough. The prisoners lost, and the lockdown in Florence, following the Marion model, continued.

Larry E. Dubois, the regional director of the Federal Bureau of Prisons who had ordered the permanent Marion lockdown, received a career advancement when Massachusetts Governor William Weld in 1991 appointed him commissioner of the state's department of corrections.

Shortly after arriving, Dubois replicated the Marion model in the Massachusetts state penitentiary's Departmental Disciplinary Unit. The ACLU sued to close it down but received a decision much like the court ruling that blessed the conditions at the federal super-max prison in Florence, Colorado.

Massachusetts, like many states, spends more on prisons and jails than it does on higher education, and prison reform to date has been a matter of semantics. Guards now are called "correctional officers"; wardens—"superintendents"; prisons—"correctional institutions"; prisoners—"inmates;" solitary confinement—"segregation"; and Walpole has been bucolically renamed Cedar Junction. The nice-sounding words have done nothing to change the reality of a harsh captivity for many and greater safety for almost no one.

Spend a moment, if you would, considering one painful and expensive irony. Courts define cruel and unusual punishment as "the infliction of pain or loss without necessity." If this definition were functional rather than theoretical, one-half of Massachusetts prisoners, *according to the department of corrections,* today would and could be safely released from their cells to less-restrictive alternatives.

For decades I have been visiting and interviewing inmates in prison, institutions separated from the outside world by high, concrete walls and even higher razor wire. The lawyers' interview room is usually buried far inside the institution. To get there you have to pass through many "traps." Walk down a corridor and a door in front of you opens; step through the opening; the door behind you closes, you are now standing in a sealed room. Wait a while. Then the door in front of you opens and you step into another corridor. The door behind you slams shut, and you walk down another corridor to another trap. Doors open. Doors close.

Some clients have been awaiting trial. Others have been serving lengthy sentences of, say, ten to twelve years. These numbers now represent actual real years to be served, but prisoners almost always would happily exchange a sentence with letters, i.e., LIFE, for a sentence with numbers, even big numbers. A first-degree murder conviction in Massachusetts means life without the possibility of parole. Second-degree murder and other crimes have a mandatory sentence of life with the possibility of parole after fifteen or twenty years of hard time. Although that possibility of parole represents light at the end of the tunnel, inmates find out that pleading their case to members of the parole board generally results in those bureaucrats lengthening the tunnel.

Clients who are locked up generally are happy to see their lawyer. We bring news from the outside. We break the routine. A lawyer visit allows time to strategize, to plan, to try to envision (without allowing the possibility to intrude into their thoughts too much) the possibility of winning. It's a time to taste, just a little, the possibility of living outside the excruciating monotony of prison.

One afternoon decades ago, while working for the Vera Institute in New York City, I accompanied Rip, one of the ex-con counselors, to see a potential client in The Tombs, the building with jail cells connected to the courthouse. As the final door of the last trap opened, Rip said, "It's still amazing to me. For years I dreamed about ways to be able to open those grates and doors. Now all I have to do," he held up his Vera identification card, "is show them this."

I don't think I'll ever forget that conversation with Rip. Everytime I walk out of a jail or prison, I give thanks that the card that got me in also worked to get me out. When driving out of a prison parking lot, an image inevitably intrudes—that of my client being returned to his cell after our visit, facing years or decades in it. And if either I or the system fails him, maybe not just years or decades, maybe forever.

The solution to the expensive insanity of prisons is no secret. In Massachusetts and across America the time has come for us to escape from the perceived political expediency of mindlessly incarcerating; to raze prisons instead of building them; and to uncage people who pose no danger. We should do this because a society wired together by prisons and police cannot flourish. We should do it because sensible penology and rational fiscal policies require it. We also should do it, in the words of the poet Diane DiPrima, "for the stars that they may look on earth and not be ashamed."

Spring 1996

Postscript

By the year 2000, America was indeed incarcerating 2,000,000 people and as of 2013, 2,400,000—at an annual average cost per prisoner of approximately $50,000. A total of 7,500,000 people are now under the control of the penal system—in prison or jail or on probation or parole. As Michelle Alexander writes in *The New Jim Crow: Mass Incarceration in the Age of Colorblindness*, "Jim Crow and slavery were caste systems. So is our current system of mass incarceration."

JFK

I remember November 22, 1963—as does everyone alive in America then.

It was a sunny Friday, and I was in the eighth grade. A woman shouted through the open doorway of our art class, "The President's been shot." A few minutes later the teacher sent us to the cafeteria. On a black-and-white TV in the front of the room Walter Cronkite was announcing the death of President Kennedy.

Let me confess. I do not cling to misty memories of Camelot. While president, JFK philandered a lot and shared a lover with a Mafia don. He lied to America about his health—his Addison's disease and venereal disease, too. And his Cold War philosophy, "We shall pay any price, bear any burden, meet any hardship ..." resulted in the first American military "advisors" being sent to Vietnam. Of course, John Kennedy did not give us the napalm and fire-bombed villages and two million casualties. Johnson and Nixon did that.

And although his phone call to Coretta Scott King when Reverend King was locked up in an Atlanta jail in 1960 garnered him the votes to win the election, for almost three years after that JFK remained a bystander in the fight for racial equality. By 1963, while still juggling the calculus of Southern segregationist Democrats controlling a lot of electoral votes, John Kennedy managed to jettison his own timidity and took to heart one of his favorite quotes based on an interpretation of Dante's *Inferno* that "the hottest places in hell are reserved for those who, in a time of great moral crisis, preserve their neutrality."

Jack Kennedy also gave us the Peace Corps, Volunteers in Service to America (VISTA), the Apollo space program, and the New Frontier, a label for his administration's domestic and foreign programs. He sought, as he pledged during his inaugural address, to "help those people in the huts and villages of half of the globe struggling to break the bonds of mass misery." He recognized the United Nations as "our last best hope in an age when the instruments of war have outpaced the instruments of peace." He concluded that memorable speech by saying, "All this will not be finished...in the life of this administration, nor even perhaps in our lifetime on this planet. But let us begin." A thousand days after he spoke those words, he was dead.

Five years after his brother's assassination, Robert Kennedy sought in his presidential campaign to resurrect his brother's political spirit. But on the night he won the California Democratic presidential primary Bobby, too, was murdered. In his eulogy for Bobby, his brother Teddy said, "My brother need not be idealized, or enlarged in death beyond what he was in life...a good and decent man, who saw wrong and tried to right it, saw suffering and tried to heal it, saw war and tried to stop it."

In 1980, Teddy ran against President Jimmy Carter for the Democratic Party nomination. Chappaquiddick hobbled him, he ran an unfocused campaign, and he lost. He deserved to. He probably should not have run at all, but he finally found his voice and purpose in the concession speech he delivered to the Democratic National Convention. There, invoking the aspirations of his brothers, he said, "For me, a few hours ago, this campaign came to an end. But for all those whose cares have been our concern, the work goes on, the cause endures, the hope still lives, and the dream shall never die."

President Kennedy's son died this week in an airplane crash. The papers say we mourn the loss of John, Jr., who wore celebrity without pretense, and I think that's true. More true is that we who remember 1963 have been picturing over and over again the photograph of three-year-old John, Jr. saluting his father's coffin on a horse-drawn caisson. We have been experiencing yet again how the assassinations of Jack and Bobby and Martin Luther King, Jr. remain sadness without solace.

July 1999

TEACH YOUR CHILDREN WELL

Recent newspaper headline: *Boomers Turning 50*. The story: Started this year, a ten-year demographic trend. Veterans came home in 1945, got married, had kids. Those kids still living are beginning to turn fifty. Are now former hippies, radicals, yippies, yuppies. Note the adjective "former."

The first lesson? Distrust adjectives. The second? Distrust news stories.

Try this version: A fair number of those World War II veterans' kids rebelled against conformity, questioned authority, got politicized, yelled "Hell no, we won't go," and didn't. Or did, and returned disaffected. Some died in The War. Some died fighting against it.

Many never went, remained unscathed, got degrees, assumed some important positions, and became policy wonks and computer mavens. Guys got their hair cut, looked respectable. Advocated environmentalism. Asserted that gay people should be treated like people. Opposed nukes. Believed in equality. Pretty much tried to practice it.

A formative moment: JFK's assassination.

John Kennedy—a promise of the best and the brightest. The Peace Corps. VISTA. He could see the light at the end of the tunnel in Vietnam.

The Civil Rights Movement—also a promise. Eradication of the ugliness and poverty in America through morality and nonviolence.

Then, the Gulf of Tonkin Resolution. The draft. The body bags.

Much of that World War II generation could not conceive of criticizing our government in time of war or believe that America could do evil. But we saw My Lai. Made us sick. Made the world sick.

On December 7, 1941—World War II began for America. Three and a half years later, it ended. We won. GIs came home. Life resumed.

The Vietnam War began consuming America in 1965. Didn't end for a decade. We lost. The troops came home. Life didn't resume as before.

Last year McNamara apologized for the deaths of 55,000 Americans and two, maybe three, million Vietnamese. Too little, very late.

Saving South Vietnam for democracy while Bull Connors' dogs sank their teeth into children and George Wallace snarled, "Segregation now, segregation tomorrow, segregation forever!"

The tension ratcheted up. Students for a Democartic Society (S.D.S.) Riots in Watts and Newark. The Black Panthers. Huey Newton, Bobby Seale, Stokely Carmichael. The Chicago police murdered Fred Hampton.

Days of rage in Chicago—and the police riot at the 1968 Democratic convention. "The police are not here to create disorder, they're here to preserve disorder." Thank you, Mayor Daley, for confirming that.

The Chicago 8 trial—Yippies Abbie Hoffman, and Jerry Rubin, Black Panther Bobby Seale, Tom Hayden and Rennie Davis from SDS, Dave Dillinger from the National Mobilization Committee. Other activists: Lee Weiner and John Froines. Kunstler defends. Judge Julius Hoffman proves Lenny Bruce right: "In the halls of justice the only justice is in the halls."

A march on Washington. Another march on Washington. The Defense Department on full alert: Yippies have announced they will levitate the Pentagon.

A moral question arose repeatedly: Do you have the guts to risk getting maced, bloodied by a police nightstick, attacked by dogs?

Agnew and Nixon declared a war. On nattering nabobs of negativism. Anyone who challenged the government.

Agnew took bribes in a brown paper bag. Nixon conspired about a bad breaking and entering, obstructed justice. They declared another war—one on crime. Exempted themselves.

But hope flowed too, sometimes. The New Frontier. Freedom Summer. A Great Society. The Civil Rights Act, and The Voting Rights Act. Later, Clean for Gene. Americans walked on the moon.

Most political people from the '60s did not cash in their values. They got out-spent, out-organized, and out-voted. Some got tired, too.

Veterans of 1960s progressive political movements do not control most levels of power. The simple reason: they're not a majority. Weren't then. Aren't now. But in concert with a new generation that holds the same values, maybe they could be.

Age fifty for parents means many of their kids are becoming adults. A thought for me and my friends: reignite those former values of the 1960s—do it with our children. Fight against racism, anti-Semitism and homophobia; pledge allegiance to each other in a fight against poverty and inequality; dedicate ourselves to preserving what remains of the earth's beauty; hold fast to the ideals of freedom of speech and religion for all people. Forget "former."

We remember the words—well, at our age, most of them anyway — to Graham Nash's "Teach Your Children Well." As the post–World War II generation begins to turn fifty, we will soon find out if we did.

March 1996

THE DEATH
PENALTY AND ME

INVITATION
TO AN EXECUTION

My co-counsel, Bryan Stevenson, and I drove south from Atlanta thirty-five miles to the Georgia Diagnostic and Classification Center, a maximum-security prison surrounded by rolling hills and manicured lawns. This is where Georgia executes inmates.

As we entered the attorneys' visiting room, I saw a young, smiling African-American man with short-cropped hair walking toward us in a Big Bird–like gait, with his hand outstretched. Bryan introduced me to Kenny Blanks, my first death row client. Bryan's clients are all on death row.

"Boy, am I glad to see you," Kenny said. At first I thought that he simply was thanking us for taking his case. Later I came to understand that he also was thanking us just for being there. Except for Bryan, he hadn't had a visit for two years.

That shouldn't have surprised me, I suppose. From the record I knew that Kenny Blanks was a tenth-grade dropout who had been shuffled from parent to stepparent to foster care to the Job Corps.

His height surprised me. According to the court records and the transcripts I read before flying to Georgia, Kenny, at the time of the crime, had just turned eighteen, tested at the maturation level of a thirteen-year-old, and was 5'10." But the young man standing in front of me clearly stood a good two or three inches taller than six feet. Prison apparently was the first time he regularly had enough to eat. Maybe that explains why he had literally grown up there.

Kenny's trip to death row began on July 26, 1983, when twenty-six-year-old Theodore Woodard, a man he'd recently met and whose apartment he moved into after he aged out of institutional care, invited him to go partying. Woodard told Kenny that he first needed to drive to Sea Island to pick up money owed him for a gardening job. Woodard had worked on the property cutting grass for a landscaping company. He was not owed anything. When William Roberts, a successful, civic-minded, recently retired corporate executive, answered the door, Woodard pulled out a pistol and bullied his way inside. Kenny followed him. He shouldn't have—perhaps a more mature person wouldn't have—but he did.

Inside, Woodard murdered Mr. and Mrs. Roberts by asphyxiating them. Woodard and Kenny left the house together but split up soon after. A day or two later, Woodard, who had stolen the Roberts's BMW, led the police on a 130-mph chase through three counties in South Georgia. As the police were about to capture him at a road block, Woodard drank the seven ounces of the weed killer paraquat that he had carried with him to the Roberts's house, then slumped into unconsciousness and died.

Kenny turned himself in and was charged with murdering Mr. and Mrs. Roberts as a joint venturer with Woodard. The jury convicted him quickly and sentenced him to death quickly as well. The Georgia Supreme Court, in affirming his conviction and death sentence, stated, "During a lengthy interrogation Blanks admitted his presence at the scene of the crime, but sought to attribute his participation to fear of Woodard." The evidence, the court ruled, "was sufficient to support the convictions" although the evidence remained unclear as to what Kenny had done.

The Georgia court system had judged Kenny a murderer who deserved to be killed by the state. To me he seemed a gentle, soft-spoken young man with a sense of humor. Outside the prison I asked Bryan a question that I had quarantined in the back of my mind but which now seemed to be demanding an answer: "If we lose, do we go to his execution?"

Bryan nodded, not so much at knowing the answer, but at knowing the question. Every volunteer Northern lawyer with whom he has worked sooner or later has asked it. Bryan understands the law of capital punishment as well as any lawyer in the country. He also knows the law of averages, which dictates that some of us Northern lawyers would see our clients killed by the state.

Until then, I hadn't really faced the possibility of witnessing an execution. Standing outside the prison, with the heat and humidity making the handle of my briefcase feel as sticky as glue, I felt a shiver run up my spine. Over the next eight years I would spend many nights pacing around my house, worrying about whether we had done everything we could and should do, whether there was anything we had overlooked that would end with us attending Kenny's execution.

Our defense team (that later included Buz Eisenberg from Ashfield, Massachusetts and Terry Jackson from Savannah, Georgia) sought relief in the Circuit Court for Glynn County, at the Georgia Supreme Court, twice at the United States Supreme Court, at the federal district court, and then in the state courts again. Ultimately we achieved a reversal of the death sentence, replaced by a sentence of life with the possibility of parole. In the death penalty world this constitutes a win, perhaps the biggest in my legal career. After all, how often do you have the chance to help save a life?

This year the Massachusetts House of Representatives voted 80 to 80 to restore capital punishment for sixteen categories of homicides, a law that would have made more than one hundred defendants per year death-eligible. That dead-even result meant the bill to reestablish capital punishment failed by one vote.

Death penalty proponents had offered a new and chilling justification for this proposed legislation. "I'm frustrated," said one of our local state representatives, Nancy Flavin, as she reversed her previous opposition to capital punishment. Her vote, she explained, provided a catharsis for her anger over three recent murders.

Our lawmakers know that the death penalty would not make us safer. Massachusetts has one of the lowest murder rates in the nation. A person is more than twice as likely to be murdered in a state with the death penalty as in a state without it. These facts are not counter-intuitive. Violence engenders more violence, particularly when the state is the perpetrator. In Massachusetts first-degree murderers must be sentenced to life without parole—in effect, to die in prison. And they do.

My friend David Hoose, a preeminent criminal defense attorney in western Massachusetts and a leading anti–death penalty advocate as well, recently wrote in a letter to the editor of the *Daily Hampshire Gazette* that murderers often offer as their excuse their own frustration—frustration about lack of respect or money, frustration at not being able to control a person or events. "How ironic," wrote Hoose, "that Rep. Flavin has based her decision on the same ground as every other person who decides to kill."

The responsibility for a death penalty system starts with the legislators who enact those statutes. When they pass a law for a new school or road or sewer plant, they can't wait to be present and have the press take their photographs at the place where their votes came to fruition. The same logic should apply here, which leads to my question for the Nancy Flavins of the Massachusetts legislature, the fifty percent who voted to reestablish capital punishment: were you planning to attend the executions?

December 1997

GEORGE BUSH
AND BILL CLINTON

Gary Graham maintained to the end that he did not commit the murder. He could not, would not, acquiesce in the state killing him. For him there would be no capitulation, no agreement, no acceptance, so he fought and flailed as guards pushed and dragged him to the death chamber in the Huntsville, Texas prison on June 22, 2000. He continued to struggle with every ounce of his strength even as the guards were strapping him onto the gurney and as they shot poison into his veins and took his life.

More troubling than the grave doubt about his guilt and his age—seventeen at the time of the crime—is that Graham was executed in the service of a political campaign. Texas Governor George W. Bush calculated that another execution on his watch certainly wouldn't hurt his run for president of the United States and a commutation might. So Graham needed to die.

But George W. Bush did not establish the precedent that it was acceptable to kill a convict to help a presidential campaign. Bill Clinton did.

In 1992, then–Arkansas Governor Clinton interrupted his campaign to return to Little Rock to preside over the execution of Ricky Ray Rector. Clinton, fearful of being portrayed as a Democrat soft on crime, saw in Rector the opportunity to prove he wasn't.

Rector had been lobotomized after he shot himself in the head in an unsuccessful suicide attempt that immediately followed his shooting and killing police officer Robert Martin. As Rector was being taken to the death chamber in Lincoln, Arkansas, he told a guard that he had saved the slice of pecan pie from his last meal and left it by his bed so that he could eat it later, after he was brought back to his cell. Then Rector was executed.

Bush claims comfort in the killing of Graham and the 134 others executed while he has occupied the governor's office because he has spent between fifteen minutes to a half hour reviewing each capital case before denying the clemency petition. That is enough time and energy, he assures us, for him to conclusively determine not only that the person committed the crime, but also that he deserves to die.

Bush's amorality is as striking as his arrogance. Texas, as he knows, has the worst capital defender system in the country. Capital case defense lawyers in Texas have slept through parts of trials and conducted cross examinations drunk. The appellate courts have held that such conduct does not deprive a defendant on trial for his life of the constitutional guarantee of effective assistance of counsel. If the lawyer comes to court and breathes, the courts have, in essence, ruled, that's good enough. Gone unspoken is that these lawyers are representing poor, usually nonwhite defendants. As governor, Bush vetoed the bill that would have established a statewide capital defender system and provided competent counsel to death-eligible defendants.

W. justifies each execution by pointing to the evidence of guilt. In Graham's case, his written rejection of clemency noted the testimony of an eyewitness who, having observed the murder from half a football field away, identified Graham as the killer. The governor made no mention that the defense lawyer never interviewed, and the jury never heard, the two much closer and credible eyewitnesses who swear that Graham was not the person who commited the crime.

Lousy lawyering in capital cases can kill a defendant in various ways. The most obvious—Graham's case stands as a good example—is the conviction of an innocent person. In other cases, a defendant should have been found guilty of committing a lesser crime such as manslaughter, but was convicted of capital murder instead.

Other defendants die because they effectively had no lawyer when their life was at stake in the penalty phase—the life or death phase—of the trial. Their lawyer didn't interview friends and family, school teachers, and coworkers who could have humanized the defendant to the jury;

didn't bother to find out if there was a neurological or psychological explanation for the crime; couldn't concern himself with uncovering the years of abuse as a child, or expend the effort to bring experts who could explain the effects of drug abuse or, sometimes, the psychosis-inducing effect of withdrawal from drugs. Juries in Texas and elsewhere often pass judgment knowing nothing about the defendant or the reason for the crime, and without being given any reason why he should be allowed to live.

Bush, in addition to killing the legislation to give capital defendants competent counsel, also killed a proposed law that would have abolished the possibility of parole for convicted murderers. That's not a misprint. Texas, *unlike* thirty other states that have capital punishment, allows the possibility of parole for first-degree murderers who escape the death penalty. Why would Bush, of all people, support the possibility of parole for murderers?

Well, he doesn't, of course. And in truth, Texas parole board members never let convicted murderers out (though theoretically they could).

Here's the political skinny: Studies show that jurors in capital cases mistakenly believe that if they sentence a defendant convicted of murder to life, he will be released on parole in a few years, so they vote for death instead. Conversely, if a judge informs jurors that the alternative to a death sentence is life without even the possibility of parole, they often refuse to impose the ultimate sentence. To look tough, Bush wants to ensure that people are executed, so he opposed a law that would have allowed juries to impose a sentence of life without parole as the alternative to death.

Bush is using his record on capital cases to win votes. And why not? Capital punishment as political expediency seems to work. Ask Bill Clinton.

October 1992

TIMOTHY McVEIGH

For years after Timothy McVeigh detonated 5000 pounds of ammonium nitrate at the Alfred P. Murrah Federal Building in Oklahoma City and killed 168 men, women, and children, a child wrote valentines to his dead mother, whom McVeigh murdered there. A boy who survived that April 1995 bombing has lived his life with a tube stuck in his throat because his ash-seared lungs cannot breathe, and we count him among the lucky. The news reports from McVeigh's trial are so disturbing, the consequences of his criminality so reprehensible and grotesque, that I've had to turn off the television or radio, put down the newspaper, and pace around the kitchen.

Tufts University professor Hugo Bedeau, an internationally respected expert on capital punishment, who I came to know when we served together on the board of Massachusetts Citizens Against the Death Penalty (MCADP), has said that McVeigh "is the kind of case where people who oppose the death penalty are willing to make an exception or are troubled by their inability to explain why they are unwilling to."

And for good reason. Most anti–death penalty arguments don't apply.

Let's start with racism. The story of capital punishment in America is frequently shown in black and white, which, for accuracy's sake, it should be. A black defendant is twice as likely to be sentenced to death than a white one. If the victim is white rather than black, the jury is four times more likely to vote for death. But McVeigh is white, so much of this argument does not apply.

Another abolitionist argument is that the legal machinery of death often produces a wrong and deadly result. Hundreds of defendants who have been found guilty beyond any reasonable doubt, had their convictions affirmed on appeal and their new trial motions and habeas corpus petitions denied, have been released from prison decades later, the courts having determined them to be innocent. Happenstance and fortuity, DNA, or a dedicated lawyer's good work have saved their lives. Other equally innocent inmates have been carried out to the prison graveyard because their time ran out. As Sister Helen Prejean puts it in *Dead Man Walking*, do you really believe that the same government that can't seem to fix a pothole should be entrusted to decide who lives and who dies?

But for Timothy McVeigh, this consideration has no relevance. The defense has virtually conceded that he committed mass murder beyond all doubt.

Some defendants are convicted of capital murder because prosecutors have suppressed evidence of innocence and mitigating information as well. However, McVeigh's prosecutor, Joseph Hartzler enjoys a reputation as a squeaky clean lawyer.

Death rows are disproportionately filled with the mentally ill, the developmentally disabled, and victims of abuse, many of whom have suffered brain injury. But McVeigh does not fall into any of these categories or suffer any of these maladies. His crime was domestic terrorism, pure and simple. He was trying to engender an uprising of the people, motivated by hatred of the government for the murder of eighty-two innocent people at the Branch Davidian compound in Waco, Texas, in 1993. McVeigh's thinking was perversely misguided, but he suffers from no recognized mental illness.

Courts often assign an inexperienced, overmatched, and incompetent lawyer to defend an accused in a capital case, but McVeigh has Stephen Jones, an excellent and experienced defense attorney. That argument against capital punishment holds no water in this case.

Whether a defendant lives or dies often appears to be no more rational than the results of a spin of a roulette wheel. A co-defendant accused in a joint venture may be more culpable but turns state's evidence and serves ten years while the other co-defendant is put to death. Here, McVeigh owns the crime, the deaths, and the suffering. He masterminded the murders and committed them. McVeigh, by all accounts, deserves to be judged far more harshly than his co-conspirator Terri Nichols, who didn't detonate the bomb and was in Kansas at home with his family when McVeigh set it off. Nichols has received 161 consecutive life-without-parole sentences. The argument of disproportionality of a death sentence doesn't help McVeigh.

Geography also often plays a part in the system. A handful of states commit eighty percent of the executions in America, and within those states a handful of counties supply the bodies that keep death rows filled. Whether or not a defendant is sent to "the row" is determined not so much by the facts of the crime he committed, but rather on which side of a county line the crime occurred. But McVeigh's is a federal prosecution. Federal prosecutors would have sought the same death penalty for this terrorist mass murderer regardless of the location of the federal courthouse he bombed.

Whether the government executes someone or not should not be determined or influenced by the expense, but some people think that the cost of keeping a murderer alive should matter, so let's take on that issue.

As a systemic matter, life imprisonment is far cheaper than state-sponsored executions. On average, it costs three to five times as much to execute someone as it does to keep him in prison for life. Timothy McVeigh, who was twenty-seven years old at the time of the crime, if he were to receive a sentence of life without the possibility of parole, could very well live for many more years. Guesswork tells us that it would cost about the same to keep him locked up for life as it would to execute him. So the usual cost savings that a life sentence brings would not be realized.

While on the subject of money, let's not forget the differences between defendants who can afford a good lawyer and those who can't. A poster in my office shows a hangman's noose about to be placed around a black man's neck, with the words underneath in a font that looks like a dictionary's. Those words define "Capital Punishment" as "Those without the capital get the punishment." But McVeigh's defense is not being hampered by lack of funds.

In sum, all these arguments against capital punishment don't mitigate against executing McVeigh.

And so, Newman, you are OK with capital punishment in his case? Sometimes I am asked this question during a death penalty panel or a speaking engagement where I am representing the ACLU or Massachusetts Citizens Against the Death Penalty. To which the answer is, "Actually, no, I'm not."

I believe that no one, least of all the government, should with pre-meditation kill another human being. By killing in our name the government exalts vengeance, demeans life, and makes us all complicit. But Professor Bedeau, for whom I have the greatest respect, apparently disagrees.

Bedeau has said, "Speaking personally, I'll let the criminal justice system execute all the McVeighs they can capture provided they'd sentence to prison all the people who are not like McVeigh. That would cover 99.9 percent of the people on death row." Of course, no politician or prosecutor is offering Professor Bedeau that deal.

The problem with America's capital punishment system is just that—it's a system. You don't get to choose the person or persons you think should die. Rather, on your and my behalf, the government has created an entire infrastructure of death, one that is broken, racist, and arbitrary, one that, because of human fallibility, inevitably makes mistakes, which is to say, it kills entirely innocent persons.

The late Supreme Court Justice Harry Blackman's was the fifth and deciding vote in the 1976 case in which the Supreme Court reinstituted the death penalty. Blackman lived to regret that vote more than any other he made as a justice. In a 1994 dissent from the court's denial of a petition to consider relief in a capital case Blackman wrote, "From this day forward, I shall no longer tinker with the machinery of death." The problem was, and is, that Harry Blackman's understanding that arbitrariness and racism constitute the foundations of our system of executions came eighteen years too late.

Given that a majority of Americans clearly no longer support capital punishment, why do death penalty verdicts still come down the assembly line?

We can attribute part of the reason to the fact that every juror in a capital case is "death qualified." This means that every prospective juror with moral scruples against capital punishment is excluded from the jury, whereas prospective jurors who favor the death penalty can serve provided they'll say that they don't believe that the death penalty *automatically* should be imposed in every homicide.

The legal rules about which prospective jurors sit on the panel put the scales of justice out of whack for another reason. Studies show that death-qualified jurors will convict far more often than jurors who oppose state-sponsored killing.

Given the 3300 men and women already sentenced to die and our rate of imposing death sentences, America could execute a prisoner every day for the next twenty years and not run out of bodies on death row. We can hope that the probable exection of the person responsible for the death, suffering, and carnage in Oklahoma City does not open the floodgates to executions across the United States. That would be a legacy of death too great even for Timothy McVeigh.

June 1997

9/11

TWO WEEKS AFTER

Street merchants were hawking "Rolex" watches for twenty dollars. Cars and trucks were crawling across midtown. In subway stations commuters were dropping dollars into the open instrument cases of accomplished guitarists and exquisite flutists.

New York City, I found, a week after 9/11, hadn't changed. Then again, it had. Images that we can't put aside have changed us all—United Airlines Flight 175 smashing into the South Tower; 110-story glass monoliths imploding; American flags flying on top of the rubble.

And this one: During the evacuation of the elementary school on Chambers Street, a second-grader looked up and, not being able to comprehend the human bodies falling from the towers, cried out, "Look, teacher, the birds are on fire!"

At a meeting in Manhattan in late September, about sixty blocks north of where the World Trade Center had stood, the first question we asked each other was not on the agenda. It was, "Did you know anyone?"

One man told us how his close friend's son walked down seventy-eight flights of the World Trade Center only to find the stairway blocked by a collapsed elevator shaft. Knowledgeable about building construction and understanding he was about to die, he managed, with a broken leg and carrying an even more injured person on his back, to crawl under the debris to an open space between cracked concrete near the street. Rescue workers pulled him out and lifted him onto a gurney and into an ambulance. Some people who he had come upon at the end of the blocked stairwell did not crawl behind him. A few minutes later, the building collapsed.

My brother works at an office on Gold Street, six blocks from the World Trade Center, his regular subway stop. Because he was running late that morning, he wasn't underneath the towers when the planes hit.

One event often shapes the perspective of a generation—the death of Franklin Roosevelt for my parents', the assassination of John Kennedy for mine. The attack on the World Trade Center compares as seminal an event for our kids.

A friend and I went to see an exhibit about 9/11 that a local principal had put up near the entrance to her school. The first graders' pictures showed persons holding candles, firefighters with rescue dogs, and people praying. In one, a plane was flying into a building. The plane and the building were about the same size. Another showed a skyscraper in the shape of an American flag. Below it were the words, "I hope they find another person alive." Another depicted a man picking up a rock. The words below explained, "My cousin is picking up a big rock on fire to help a guy trapped underneath."

Many fifth-graders wrote poems. The one titled "Tragic Times" expressed this thought: "Imagine being one of the workers of the World Trade Center...a mom going to work...imagine the kids waiting for your mom to come and pick you up...." Another consists of an eight-word sentence: "No fear will keep tears away for days." Many poems are acrostics. One said:

N

Empty Spaces

W

Y

O

R

K

After my meeting I met my daughter Jo, who is nineteen and a student at the Tisch School at NYU, and took her for dinner at the Pig 'n' Whistle, a busy Irish pub. When she and I walked past Engine Company 65, near Times Square, some of the thousands of flowers were wilting on the sidewalk in front, but many were fresh. Some of the pictures of the missing taped to the building were folded and crumpled a bit, but we could still read the words: "Last seen—82nd floor, World Trade Center, 10:05 a.m., September 11, 2001." There were hundreds of flags, hundreds of pictures. I took off my hat. We stood there in silence.

The day after the attack, the principal at another local elementary school had the students assemble in the cafetorium. She then asked all the staff—teachers, counselors, custodians, office and cafeteria workers, the nurse—to join her in forming a circle around the kids. She told them that all these adults were in the school to help them, to teach them, and to keep them safe.

Kids will not forget the horror of September 11. Nor should they. But if they retain, and we nurture, the sense of sharing that has—for the moment anyway—enveloped the country, they will have been given an invaluable lesson about the possibility of courage and the importance of community—lessons that would honor 3000 lives and 3000 deaths.

October 2011

AT WHAT COST?

Our country is not as free as it was eight days ago because President Bush has signed into law the USA Patriot Act, which passed the United States Senate 98 to 1 and the House of Representatives 357 to 66.

This legislation does contain a few sensible provisions such as those prohibiting money-laundering in offshore banks. But primarily it fosters governmental suppression of dissent, legitimizes unnecessary surveillance of law-abiding citizens, and allows for the imprisonment and deportation of *legal* immigrants for little or no reason.

Let's start with suppression of dissent. The September 11 attacks violated three separate federal anti-terrorism laws that carry the death penalty. Nonetheless, the USA Patriot Act creates a new and unnecessarily broad definition of domestic terrorism—as "activities that involve *acts dangerous to human life* that are a violation *of any* [state or federal criminal] *law* [and] *appear to be intended* ... to influence the policy of a government by intimidation or coercion ...."

Notice that "any" violation of the law can trigger the definition. Disturbing the peace? Assault and battery? An alleged conspiracy to commit these crimes?

Don't ignore that the acts must only "appear" to be intended to influence the government by intimidation or coercion. How a protest appears to a federal prosecutor may vary enormously from the perspective of a political activist.

"Acts dangerous to human life" might mean sitting down in front of a car. "By intimidation or coercion?" The government reflexively views challenges to its authority as intimidating.

Persons associated with organizations as diverse as Operation Rescue and the Environmental Liberation Front, as well as protestors at the World Trade Organization meetings, have engaged in activities that might put them in the dock as accused terrorists facing draconian penalties.

We used to believe that the First Amendment right to gather together to petition or protest against the government constituted a hallmark of our democracy. Apparently, no longer—or at least, not so much.

As for surveillance, the law gives the FBI and other federal agencies greater rights to wiretap phones and monitor e-mails while at the same time stripping courts of much of their traditional authority to rein in and prevent unconscionable intrusions into our personal liberty. The bill also sanctions law enforcement access to an individual's medical and financial records without the person's knowledge or consent.

There's more.

Until last week federal law provided that academic, disciplinary, and financial records of college students were confidential. Now institutions of higher education must turn over student information to the FBI any time that the bureau, without any meaningful judicial review, asserts that a student's record is "relevant" to an investigation.

And more.

Before the USA Patriot Act became law, over 1000 persons had been—and they remain—locked up on material witness warrants and pretextual immigration charges. The act increases the government's ability to detain noncitizens indefinitely.

The rationale for the legislation, regardless of how unnecessary, ineffective, and intrusive some provisions are, at least would be understandable if these expanded powers applied strictly to anti-terrorism efforts. But they don't. These powers apply to routine criminal investigations, as well.

In instances when the Department of Justice still must receive judicial authorization to spy on its citizens, the FBI now can receive permission from a secret court created by the Foreign Intelligence Surveillance Act of 1978. Russ Feingold, the one U.S. senator who voted against the bill, has characterized the court as "the Attorney General's private playground."

The history of America's responses to both perceived and real foreign threats provides little comfort. Consider the Palmer Raids after World

War I, the internment of Japanese-Americans during World War II, the execution of Julius and Ethel Rosenberg during the Cold War, and the surveillance and infiltration of peace groups during and after Vietnam.

We, of course, cannot predict with certainty how the new law will be used by federal prosecutors and law enforcement agencies. We do know the predilections of the CIA and FBI when given vast powers—and their frightening histories.

At the previous zenith of its authority and discretion, the CIA, for example, assassinated the democratically elected president of Chile, Salvador Allende, and installed as dictator General Augusto Pinochet. Similarly, when the FBI had comparable, unchecked powers, it created Cointelpro. Cointelpro, an acronym for Counterintelligence Program, extinguished the Black Panther Party and infiltrated, maligned, disrupted, and destroyed many progressive and peace groups opposed to government policies.

We may take some solace in the fact that the USA Patriot Act contains a "sunset" provision. In four years, the electronic surveillance parts of the law will expire unless renewed by Congress. Four years is a long time to suspend freedom.

I agree—I think we all agree—that America should not accede to terrorism. Our elected officials espouse this theory loudly and often, but they promote it blindly and thus practice it badly.

Our nation could characterize the unnecessary loss of freedom as a casualty of the war against terrorists, but blaming terrorists would abdicate our responsibility. Terrorists cannot make America less free. Only Americans can do that.

November 2001

BIG BROTHER GEORGE

*[A] colored poster... depicted simply an enormous
face... BIG BROTHER IS WATCHING YOU, the
caption beneath it ran.*

George Orwell, *Nineteen Eighty-Four*

Last weekend President George Bush announced in fractured English
that "Anyone who espouses a philosophy that's terrorist and bent, I as-
sure you, we will bring that person to justice."

Really? Bring to justice—this president's usual euphemism for a
death sentence? Does Bush actually intend to criminalize First Amendment–protected speech?

Well, maybe. We can't know because the president's aides refused to
elaborate on this apparently unscripted pronouncement.

We do know that Bush, using the September 11 attacks as justification, pushed through Congress a series of laws collectively called the
USA Patriot Act. USA Patriot is an acronym for Uniting and Strength-
ening America by Providing Appropriate Tools Required to Intercept and
Obstruct Terrorism.

The act allows law enforcement officials to rummage around in private lives without probable cause and without judicial oversight. It in-
vests in federal prosecutors and police forces—the DOJ, FBI, CIA, DEA,
INS, among others—enormous new powers to surveil, wiretap, spy on,
detain, and imprison both citizens and noncitizens. The law allows the
government to delve into the computer files, e-mails, and internet usage
of a person whom a prosecutor—not a judge—claims may have information "relevant to an on-going investigation." The act permits the government not only to conduct unannounced and undisclosed searches in

certain circumstances, but also to help itself, through computer searches and subpoenas, to previously privileged medical, educational and financial records.

This legislation chills First Amendment freedoms to speak and write. Many of us will decline to attend a rally or sign a petition or send an e-mail or visit a website if we think that act may cause the government to target us. It is only human to try to protect ourselves—to avoid the possibility of being indicted or blacklisted.

And note this: In order for the USA Patriot Act to successfully squelch opposition to government policies, the FBI need not actually read all, or even most, computer files. When individuals fear being surveilled, the government can rely on the fact that many will simply censor themselves. As Orwell wrote in *Nineteen Eight-Four*:

> *How often ... the Thought Police plugged in on any*
> *individual wire was guesswork.... There was of course*
> *no way of knowing whether you were being watched*
> *at any given moment.*

President Bush and Attorney General John Ashcroft already have predicted that the War on Terrorism will last at least a decade. *The New York Times* reported this week that the United States now "is preparing a military presence in Central Asia that could last for years...." And according to the Bush Administration, we need to suspend freedom of speech and freedom from unreasonable searches and seizures at least for the duration of the wars.

These official pronouncements and recent developments in Central Asia bring to mind another part of *Nineteen Eight-Four*. In that novel, the enemy changes from time to time—sometimes it's Eastasia, sometimes Eurasia—but the war itself never ends.

Today's war in Afghanistan so far has cost blessedly few American lives. But this fortunate fact itself conjures another passage from Orwell.

> *[I]n a physical sense war involves very small numbers*
> *of people, mostly highly trained specialists, and causes*
> *comparatively few casualties. The fighting, when*
> *there is any, takes place on the vague frontiers whose*
> *whereabouts the average man can only guess at....*

Since September 11, thousands of immigrants have been herded into prison. The charges against them are secret; their names, for the most part, appear on no court docket; and the Bush Administration agrees they are not terrorists. They are locked up nonetheless. In addition, the FBI has been interrogating another 5000 recent immigrants based on racial and ethnic profiling. Law enforcement in America in 2002 is emulating Orwell's *Nineteen Eight-Four.*

> *Foreigners... were a kind of strange animal. One*
> *literally never saw them except in the guise of*
> *prisoners, and even as prisoners one never got more*
> *than a momentary glimpse of them. Nor did one know*
> *what became of them....*

The Bush Administration has responded to the criticism that it is mortgaging our freedoms by pointing to and celebrating the president's ninety percent approval rating. Bush's popularity correlates with the polls demonstrating that a majority of Americans will willingly forfeit fundamental freedoms if our government asserts that doing so will help defeat our enemies. Of course, in Orwell's world the government enjoyed virtually unanimous support, too.

The president's disregard for personal freedom may inflict great damage on the democratic experiment called America, but if we forfeit our freedoms, our complacency will equally be to blame. Last week in preparation for teaching a high school class that had been reading *Nineteen Eight-Four,* I reread the novel. I had forgotten the ending. Do you remember?

> *[I]t was all right, everything was all right, the struggle*
> *was finished. He had won the victory over himself. He*
> *loved Big Brother.*

January 2002

TEENAGE
DAUGHTERS

THE FIREFLIES OF JULY

I miss the fireflies of July. A secret galaxy born from the still, overflowed waters of the Connecticut River in the Meadows section of Northampton, they dance up the hillsides bounding the floodplain into the night sky. For years we have visited the fireflies on our daughter Leah's birthday, but not this year. On July 8, she turned ten—old enough for sleep-away camp, old enough to be away on her birthday, she said.

Fifty years ago cows grazed on these hills that now are blanketed with sensitive and maidenhair ferns, jackweed and jewelweed, honeysuckle, morning glories, thistle, and asters. The shrubs, flowers, and ferns live under a canopy of black and yellow birch, gray ash, silver maples, and an occasional shagbark hickory and black walnut tree. Though the farmers still work the acres below—planting corn and potatoes, mostly—they long ago gave up the cows.

A little over a month ago, we joined friends and neighbors who, like us, were strolling down toward the Meadows to visit the fireflies. Those peridot points looked like a trail of flickering light connecting earth to the rest of the Milky Way. A grape taste floated in the air from vines wending around the bark of trees. Our golden retriever, along for the walk, meditated on the soft, spongy, canine-salivated ecstasy of her tennis ball.

We pooled our knowledge about fireflies, which didn't amount to much: A chemical reaction causes the light. They're classified as beetles, not flies. Glow worms are females without wings. They don't live long, and they light to find a mate. Given their brightness, we joked that this year seemed to be a particularly romantic one.

By this time in August, Sirius' rising and setting no longer is synchronized with the sun's; the calendar stands closer to the autumnal equinox than to the summer solstice; and the fireflies are gone. The golden retriever on her nightly walk still happily absconds with one of the tennis balls stashed on our route, but now, after firefly season, we pay more attention to her, and she often drops the ball at our feet and wants to play.

When Leah was younger, she would delay bedtime by plaintively asking me to "tell a story about when you were a kid." That request was tough to turn down. I almost always joined the conspiracy to continue her day. I found that I liked telling her my stories that included, it turned out, many about summers.

I told her happy stories, funny tales, goofy things that her father or other relatives had said or done when we were kids—playing Whiffle ball with my older brother, her Uncle Jeffrey, with him having to bat lefty to make the game closer; another time, my sneaking peanut butter and jelly sandwiches to him after he ran away from home—he was hiding behind the big rock across the street, having once again broken a pane of glass playing stick ball with me; many times giving our golden retriever, Taffy, a bone and watching her bury it in the garden, then digging it up and giving her the same bone and then doing all this all over again. I omitted, of course, any sad parts—my parents' (her grandparents') divorce when I was nine, or my being shipped away to prep school, or later feeling lost at college. As the poet Patricia Schneider writes, "We make collages of the way / it might have been / had it been as we remembered, / as we think perhaps it was…."

Telling these stories about my childhood and hearing Leah's responses made me appreciate that a kid's intuition about what is fair and right may well be a better barometer of truth than any adult analysis. Stories about kids often feel more immediate and universal than our adult ones, which frequently, even at their most significant, amount only to obituary fodder.

Summer makes parents take stock of their kids, forces us to acknowledge how much they have changed since the summer before, focuses the fact that they are too quickly (if at other times, in other ways maddeningly slowly) growing up. Even for the Peter Pan–enthralled 1960s generation, the eyes of summer see that we are getting older, that nothing lasts forever. These hot and slow days offer adults respite from routinized, yet often uncalm, lives and grant parents the luxury of being together with our kids—in Schneider's words—"taking the long way home."

We all want our kids to have great summers filled with adventures and challenges and friends. We hope to provide a reservoir of stories so that they, too, can easily acquiesce to postponing bedtime when their child says, "Tell me a story about when you were a kid."

If Leah is lucky enough to have a child who graces life and loves stories as much as she does, I hope she will tell about visiting the fireflies every year on her birthday. She will leave out the part that we only did that for a while.

August 1996

READY OR NOT

I can still conjure the feeling of carrying Jo—all six-pounds-one-and-a-half ounces of her—cradled to my chest, her eyes closed, lips pursed, her head, with a few wisps of red hair, in my palm—up the back porch stairs when Dale and I brought her home from the hospital. We introduced her to the golden retriever, Caboose, who sniffed her thoroughly, licked her twice, and immediately took up residence by her bassinete. He, too, felt the need to protect her.

That was fourteen years ago. When I recently complained to a friend who has kids older than mine about my daughters' childhoods speeding by (our younger daughter Leah turned eleven this summer), he consoled me—sort of—by saying, "The first twelve or so years of parenthood pass awfully quickly, but they're averaged out by the teenage years, which generally feel interminable."

To try to get me though these years, I recently have invested in some books, my favorite being psychologist Anthony Wolf's *Get Out of My Life, but First Could You Bring Me and Cheryl to the Mall.*

Wolf emphasizes the inevitability of conflict between teenagers and their parents, pointing out the cruel irony at work. Kids want to establish their independence, but parents—reasonably enough—don't want to cede autonomy at exactly the time when the risks rise dramatically. Our fears are real. As a criminal defense lawyer, I have represented many teenagers, some of whom have almost died from heroine and cocaine, others who have killed a friend, often a best friend, in a car accident. Few cases are as sad.

Wolf's exposition brought me back to a passage in Jon Krakauer's *Into the Wild*, the story of a young man who died living his dream of trying to survive in the Alaska wilderness. Krakauer writes, "Engaging in risky behavior is a right of passage in our culture no less than in most others. Danger has always had a certain allure. That, in large part, is why so many teenagers drive too fast and drink too much and take too many drugs, why it has always been so easy for nations to recruit young men to go to war."

Girls generally don't face death in the military, but they do encounter other threats from what Mary Pipher, in *Reviving Ophelia*, calls a girl-damaging society. For girls, to the list of ever-present threats from cars and drugs we must add pernicious psychological ones such as anorexia and bulimia, and sexual issues including harassment, assault, and pregnancy. In addition, gender stereotypes that inappropriately embolden boys surreptitiously silence girls. Advertising, schools, and peers can conspire to stop them from becoming astronauts and brain surgeons. Although I have no particular reason to worry about any of these things, I worry about all of them anyway.

But count me lucky. Notwithstanding the realistically long list of my shortcomings as a father, my kids, one way or another, seem to have internalized a strong sense of self. They're great kids—smart, talented, and loving—something I need to remind myself when they act like adolescents. That said, kids and life, of course, come with no guarantees, and so I share the feeling of the mother in Pipher's book who says of her daughter, "I wish I could wrap a magic blanket around her that would keep her safe."

Every year on an August night, Dale and I take the kids to a mountain clearing where we take in the galaxies and catch the shooting stars. This year as I lay on our old blanket under the sky, I kept turning over in my mind another part of Pipher's book, the final line in a mother's poem to her daughter: "I hurl you into the universe—and pray."

September 1997

MR. PETCEN'S PUMPKINS

Thanks to Jo, age fourteen, and Leah, eleven, who both wanted to find Halloween pumpkins, we met Paul Petcen, who has lived on Chestnut Street in the small neighboring town of Hatfield for all of his eighty-one years.

From Northampton on a picture-postcard, leaves-turning, New England fall Sunday we avoided the cars crawling centipede-like on Interstate 91 and instead took Route 5 to North Hatfield. After we turned right onto Chestnut Street, we saw no other car on the road.

From a distance, the pumpkins—which we were about to find out were Mr. Petcen's—looked like giant orange mushrooms sprouting on a lawn. We drove towards them and pulled up to a farm stand piled high with squashes—butternut and buttercup, red kiri, orange Hopi, dumpling, gold nugget and acorn—names we soon would learn. A few blue-grey ones, the color and shape of a meteorite, were interspersed among them. The stem of the butternut squash, we would soon discover, smells like peanut shells.

Mr. Petcen, a little portly and younger-looking than his age, with white hair peeking out from under a baseball cap, greeted us. He had a swaying gait that resembled one of the maple leaves falling near him. A little lumbago, I guessed. I pointed to the meteorite squashes. "Hubbards," Mr. Petcen told me. "Make a delicious pie. They have a lot of meat."

The wooden cart also held peppers—giant cayennes and habaneras, as well as Bosc pears and red and yellow apples, and cherry tomatoes. No, he wasn't worried about the possible light frost predicted for that night. The canopy of the maple, which gives shade in the summer, provides protection from frost in the fall, he explained.

As Mr. Petcen replenished the cart from the rinsing tub behind him, he allowed that he didn't do as much of the farm work as he used to. His sons and their families help a lot. "They do the heavy work. I do the heavy looking-on," he told us.

I felt bad that we seemed to be the only customers. "Sometimes I get one customer," Mr. Petcen mused. "Sometimes I don't get any." Then he added, "If I was on Route 5 and 10, I could sell ten times as much."

He states this matter-of-factly, as if weighing an idea on a scale—but not envious about the idea of selling ten times as much from somewhere else. Ten or fifteen years ago Mr. Petcen took his crops to the Amherst Common Market, but he stopped because "It got to be too much picking." Now he sells only from his stand. His son Dick, who had joined our little group, told us that the produce that his dad doesn't sell they'll bring to the Food Bank, a local hunger-relief agency.

We are standing a couple hundred yards down the street from the family homestead where Mr. Petcen was born in 1916. His father farmed the four acres behind the homestead. His son and daughter-in-law, Tom and Jo Ann, now own that land and farm there. They, in turn, plan to deed it some years from now to their son. Mr. Petcen has lived at his present address on Chestnut Street for the past fifty-seven years.

Mr. Petcen cannot remember a time when he didn't farm somewhere on Chestnut Street. The few acres behind the house, of course, never yielded enough profit for him and his wife, Marcella, to live on. He worked as a machinist at Osly and Whitney in Westfield for many years and retired when he was sixty-five.

In addition to the pumpkins and corn and cabbage and squash and tomatoes, the Petcens have grown and sold what they call "everlasting flowers." Some are perennials—yarrow and baby's breath. Some are annuals—statice and celosia. They cut the flowers at maturity, when the bud is the right size, and then place the flowers in a solution of water and glycerin. Glycerin maintains the color and keeps them supple. After the flowers dry, they tie a bunch together.

"Beautiful," he said. "They are beautiful. My wife was in charge of the bouquets. There are a lot of half-made ones in the storage shed." Then he stopped. Suddenly he looked disturbingly tired. He said, "I'm about all talked out."

But he went on, lowering his voice, leaning over the peppers. "I spent the morning crying my eyes out in our church," meaning the nearby Lutheran congregation. "My wife passed on a little over a week ago."

Dale and I told him how sorry we were. "These things happen," he replied. They had been married for fifty-eight years. "We're so very sorry," we told him again.

The girls, who had been at a table some distance away, came over to the cart where we were standing and placed their gourds and small pumpkins and miniature Indian corn next to a watermelon-looking, square squash that Dale had picked out. Mr. Petcen told us it is called a stripetti. The girls then went back to a pile of pumpkins, hoisted up the ones they had chosen, and came back to the cart.

"Like that pumpkin?" I asked Leah.

"Love this pumpkin, Dad."

"Jo?"

"So cool!"

"Dale—are we all set?"

"We are."

Paul Petcen surveyed our purchases. He tapped the pumpkins with two fingers and commented that they'd make good pies as well as good jack-o'-lanterns. He said that all together the cost would be, he paused as if doing the addition in his head, eight dollars.

"Are you sure that's enough?" I asked, "It doesn't really seem like enough."

"Well, it's the end of the season," he replied.

Then he looked again at the girls, who were holding their oversized pumpkins for him to appraise, prizes they had found.

"I was right," Mr. Petcen continued. "It's enough."

October 1997

SOMETIMES, SHE'S PUFFY

Puffy, my almost fifteen-year-old daughter Jo's chestnut Quarter Horse, has an alias. Puffy boards at the Rauscher family's Heritage Farm, where Jo, who jettisoned the name Joanna when she was three or four, has been riding since she was five.

When Puffy arrived at Heritage, Maureen Rauscher asked her then-four-year-old niece Annie if she wanted to name the new horse. Annie, who was standing on the bench of the picnic table near the stable, pushed the white snip on the mare's nose, felt her exhale warm air, and said, "She's Puffy."

"That's probably not her name," Maureen responded. But the little girl knew a Puffy when she saw one, and the name stuck.

Some years later, when Maureen was married and expecting her first child, she needed to sell Puffy to raise some additional money for the home she and her husband David were building near the barn. She also needed to trust Puffy's new owner. Puffy became Jo's, though the horse never left her home at the Rauscher's barn.

Jo and Puffy together learned about, and came to love, the show event called Gambler's Choice—a competition where each rider sets her own course and sprints over as many jumps as possible within the allotted time. A typical Gambler's Choice works like this:

At the start signal Puffy, with Jo glued to the saddle, breaks toward the brick wall; 1100 pounds of horse and rider fly over it. Although Puffy is only fifteen hands, she clears that jump by a foot or more.

Puffy then gallops toward a three-foot-high picket fence. Jo's hands rest an inch or two above Puffy's withers and barely move. As they take off, Jo squeezes her right calf and almost imperceptibly pulls back her right shoulder.

Puffy responds by performing a flying lead change while over the jump. On the landing she buttonhooks, then races over the oxer, and next spins through a hairpin turn to face the natural gate. In midair over the gate, Jo studies the angle needed to jump the hedge, and Puffy does another flying lead change. They take the hedge, the brush, and the roll-top in quick order and then, from the opposite side, soar over the brick wall again.

They stop reluctantly when the buzzer sounds. Puffy has gone flat out, jumped big, and shown why, among horse people, Quarter Horses are known for having a deep heart.

Jo dismounts, removes her helmet, and hugs her horse. From a distance, it's hard to tell what's Jo's hair and what's Puffy's mane because they're the same copper color.

Jo is still flying, still flowing, chatting nonstop with her friends and fellow riders. It's hard to believe that this is the same grumpy teenager whose monosyllables pass for conversation on school-day mornings.

Quarter Horses, because they can accelerate quickly, were bred originally for western ranch work. Jo at times has swapped her English saddle for western gear and entered Puffy in team penning competitions, where three wranglers try to cut from the rest of the herd the calves whose numbers have been called, and pen them. The fastest team wins.

In past summers, when the announcer has blared, "When you're ready," Jo and her friends Val, riding Calvin, and Katie, on Tiger, have gone whooping and hollering and charging into the herd, chased the calves into the pen, and tried to block them from scooting back to join the other dogies. But they won't this coming summer. It's expensive to keep cows, and the Rauschers recently sold the herd.

These girls, who ride hard at Heritage, also work hard there. They clean tack, muck stalls, assist the ferrier and vet, and feed, water, and groom the barn's Appaloosas and pintos, bays and sorrels, thoroughbreds and Shetlands, as well as the occasional donkey and llama. They also show the transient horses and ponies offered at auctions.

But let's not overstate the case for teenage responsibility.

One spring Sunday afternoon, while driving Jo back from her friend Gillie's, she told me they had been riding Gillie's horse, Buzzie, in the fields behind the house. That sounded reasonable enough. Months later it slipped out that, unbeknownst to any adult, they had been cantering Buzzie bareback—while riding backwards together, hanging on to him and each other, facing his tail.

Nor should we brag too much about Puffy's professionalism. Non-jumping events sometimes bore her and she does not go well. And this mare enjoys—I use "enjoys" advisedly—a bad reputation for nipping and kicking geldings who graze too close to her. Of course, when she sees Jo, carrot in hand, coming to get her in the field, she whinnies.

After every ride, whether on trails or in the show ring, Jo walks and cools off Puffy. Puffy then follows Jo—the halter and lead rope are unnecessary—back into the barn with its familiar smells of hay and mash, sawdust and manure, saddles and saddle soap.

Just past the tack room, near the entrance to the indoor ring, Jo often finds and pets the calico kitten curled on a barrel top. Grover, the grey cattle dog, an Australian Blue Heeler, always strolls over for some attention. Jo puts Puffy in her stall, picks her hooves, brushes her, and makes sure she has plenty of water, bedding, and hay.

For Dale and me, it's amazing how neat Puffy's stall is. For many years we've given Jo a birthday card that says on the cover, "We wish you as much happiness as there are stars in the sky and sand on the beach." On the inside it says, "And clothes on your floor."

On the brass plate tacked to her stall, Puffy's name appears over Jo's. In bigger letters above "Puffy" is her registered name, the name by which she is introduced when she and Jo enter the show ring, the name by which this horse is known to the rest of the world. Puffy's other name is "YouBetchaBabe."

March 1998

A PUFFY ADDENDUM

Maureen's daughter Mackenzie was the child who caused Maureen and her husband David to build a house, with the result that Puffy became Jo's. After high school, when Jo moved to New York City to attend an acting conservatory, we sold Puffy back to Maureen so that Puffy could become Mackenzie's.

For five or six years Mackenzie rode and jumped Puffy and mucked her stall and fed her hay and oats. She, too, loved that horse. But a Quarter Horse generally lives about twenty, maybe twenty-five years, and Puffy was growing old.

Her arthritis became increasingly severe, and after some time no amount of supplements or vet visits, painkillers, massage, physical therapy, or ointments made her feel better. Towards the end, she would stand on three legs because the fourth hurt so much. Then she would put down that leg and wince and raise another, which also throbbed when she put weight on it.

The Rauchers are horse people. They know deep in their bones that a horse shouldn't have to live with unremitting pain. Besides, Puffy was too good and loyal to be allowed to suffer.

When they put Puffy down, Maureen and Mackenzie cried for a long time. When I told Jo the news, she did too. But I also passed along to Jo something else Maureen had told me—that they had buried Puffy in one of her favorite places, in the field behind the barn near the wood rail fence where the summer sun seems to set, the place where Puffy knew the geldings would leave her alone, where Jo, walking with carrots in hand, often would find her.

THE BROAD BRUSH STROKES

The painting consisted of two waveshaped watercolor brushstrokes—one a spectrum of purple—orchid or thistle melding into mulberry, then to lilac and violet; and below it, a second brushstroke consisting of a continuum of blue, from light to dark—turquoise and teal morphing into cerulean and cornflower and ending with the thinnest hint of midnight. Underneath, graceful calligraphy said, "The only things that parents should give children are roots and wings."

For five years that painting, a present from our friend Lynn to celebrate Jo's birth, hung in the doorway to Jo's bedroom. Ultimately the picture turned into part of a pile of ashes after our nook-filled Victorian home burned down, a fire in which, blessedly, no one was hurt.

We rebuilt the house much as it was, and for years afterward, when I'd walk past the place where that painting used to be, I thought about it. But in truth, I miss it less now because, notwithstanding the elegance of both the calligraphy and the aphorism, I think it's wrong.

Parents, I've decided, cannot give kids wings—although we can rush to provide a full-length mirror so that they can see and celebrate them when they begin to sprout. And we can't actually give them roots either. Like vegetables or flowers or anything else, once kids start growing, they're pretty much on their own. Besides, roots are particularly tricky to appraise. You cannot see how deep they are or where they've spread, and you don't know whether they are strong enough to weather a storm until after the storm.

My teenage daughters and their friends, unlike their mothers at that age, play All-Star baseball and Suburban League basketball and soccer and tennis, go after state championships, swim in tournaments, and climb mountains. They win commendations in school for excellence in technology and prove themselves whizzes at math.

For garden-variety, coming-into-adolescence girls born in the 1980s, this is how the world is, how it is supposed to be. They have few historical reference points on feminism. They do not realize that in the fight for gender equality they are radicals, revolutionaries. They take for granted, they assume and presume, a world their mothers only dreamed of. They find nothing unusual in women being Olympic stars and believe that, of course, women can be governors, senators or president, and CEOs.

There is no sense being Pollyannaish. Soon enough, our daughters and their friends will encounter gender inequality in employment, sports, and relationships, too. Nonetheless, faced with discrimination, their assumptions about life and equality should prove helpful. These daughters, in overcoming bias and stereotypes, will succeed far more and far better than their parents, who were taught Icarus too much as parable and not enough as myth.

For a present for her fifteenth birthday, Jo wants a poster that she can hang in her room next to the one of basketball star Sheryl Swoopes. She told me I could find it at the Runners' Shop downtown—a wide-angle view of NBA star Michael Jordan with his arms outstretched, a wingspan of almost seven feet. Jo also said—she was clear about this—that underneath him are the words, "No bird soars too high that soars with its own wings."

When I went to buy the poster, I found that the quote at the bottom, from William Blake, actually is gender specific and male. The words below Michael Jordan are, "No bird soars too high if *he* soars with *his* own wings." Jo didn't read it that way. Neither do her friends. Neither will her sister.

July 1998

THE NEXT SUMMER'S FIREFLIES

Leah and I were being poky. On the dirt road near our house, heading toward the Meadows and the Arcadia Wildlife Sanctuary, we'd stop every few steps to try to take in the thousands of fireflies glowing over the Japanese knotweed and alighting on the maidenhair ferns. Casey, our somewhat arthritic golden retriever, considered the pace perfect.

It had rained earlier that mid-July evening, and the sky had cleared, but it still felt muggy. A few mosquitoes pricked my neck and landed on Leah's legs, but they weren't bothering us much. It was quiet, the leaves of the beech, hemlock, and hickories silencing all but a meager hum from an occasional car on the interstate. From a stagnant, newly-formed pond nearby, a bullfrog was belching into the night. Across the valley a waxing, rising half-moon was silhouetting the Holyoke Range. The nebula looked like lace, and stars were shining into our arbor.

It was the time for fireflies. From a clearing above the floodplain, they looked like entwined garlands of small sparks. Then, jiggled by the wind, they transformed into a snake dance of oscillating lights, ebbing and flowing through the bracken and the bittersweet, rising and falling on the thermals from the bogs and the breeze off the Connecticut. As in summers past, we felt as if we were standing in the midst of galaxies.

Leah and I were each carrying a clear plastic container. We'd capture a few fireflies, then set them free.

"Look how bright these two lightning bugs are," I said as I held my jar up, their blinking reflecting off my recently acquired bifocals.

"You know," Leah replied, "the twinkling with their tails is a mating ritual."

"I know that," I replied.

"So, Dad," she said, "maybe you should give them some privacy."

Leah was laughing. Leah is twelve.

But now August has come. The fireflies, which appear almost alchemically in early July, have disappeared as if drawn behind a sorcerer's screen. Over the years I think I've noticed that fireflies rise higher in the sky near the end of their season. Minute Icaruses of the coal-black summer sky, they hover closest to the stars just before they descend back to the earth. Within a day or two of their most majestic show, they're gone.

With the advent of August both girls have taken off on their own adventures—with friends and grandparents. The house is quiet. I find myself talking more than usual to the dog, the cat, and the guinea pig. I've even driven to the barn to chat with Jo's mare.

On our once-again pedestrian nightly walks, the golden retriever moseys along and often lags behind. When I arrive at the dark field that recently was the fireflies' dance hall, I feel as if I've opened a bright birthday package only to find an empty box. That empty-box feeling reminds me of the title of a collection of poetry by Northampton attorney and social worker Sandra Goldsmith, who died three years ago at age fiftyfour. Her family titled her book *The Presence of Absence*.

September 1998

HOMEWORK HELP

"Pick an appliance, any appliance, a device, and explain how it works." That was the JFK Middle School science assignment. Leah picked the television. She asked me to explain as best I could how televisions work.

So I did. I told her everything I knew: when the clicker breaks, you have to buy a new one because they're cheap and no one repairs them.

"Sorry, okay, more seriously. Television? It's an incredible gizmo. No question about it. I remember our first black-and-white one." My mind wandered to watching *The Mickey Mouse Club* and secretly falling in love with Annette Funicello. Most men born between 1945 and 1955 will swear that at least eighty percent of what gets them in trouble with women can be attributed to Annette Funicello's early development. "Television can make you fall in love," I reported to Leah ambiguously.

"Maybe I should have picked the telephone and not the television," Leah replied.

"I remember a lot about telephones," I said helpfully. "I remember phones when you picked the receiver up and talked to the operator to make a call.

"My dad—your grandfather, Grandpa Mick—used to call his mom and dad every Sunday morning," I continued. "Their telephone number was BU-8-9795, *BU* as in short for Butterfield, but Grandpa Mick would always tell the operator that he wanted to be connected with Butter*ball* 8-9795." And the operator would invariably say, "That's Butter*field*, Sir" and he would always respond, "I would prefer if you dialed Butter*ball*, please."

"That's it?" Leah demanded to know. "That's all?"

"No, no. Not all all." I assured her. "I have more about phones. I remember as a kid being at the florist with your Granny Carole and being mystified by the sign that said, "Send Flowers By Wire." For the life of me, I couldn't figure out how those roses wouldn't end up utterly mashed after being pushed and pulled through the wires.

"Maybe we should go back to television," Leah suggested. "Seriously."

"For me," I said, "television is magic."

"No prob, dad," Leah said as she bolted for the door.

But there was a problem. I could feel the pity. Don't you just hate it when the kids pity you? I do. So to make sure nothing like this happens again, I've been spending time examining the blender and have a half-dozen smoothie recipes all ready to go.

October 1998

CONSIDERING DANDELIONS

It was early. The sunlight through the blinds had formed a picket fence of shadow and light on my desk. Seeing some full-blown dandelions and remnants of others on the lawn outside my study window at home stirred a forty-year-old memory.

I was eight, maybe nine, years old and sitting at the kitchen table when my mother informed me that dandelions were not flowers, but weeds. I remember feeling angry and actually not believing her. Dandelions were beautiful, particularly in bunches, and magical, too. After the blossoms disappeared, you could use them to make wishes and then trust the wind to carry their tops to somewhere those wishes might come true. Weeds, on the other hand, were ugly and unwanted, something to be rooted out and tossed away. At nine years old, I had no doubt—a dandelion was a flower.

That memory sent me to my bookshelves to find a poem by Greg Orr, the first real poet I ever met. In 1970 he and I and several other Antioch College students shared a house—a brick, two-story, 200-year-old former tavern and inn in Clifton, Ohio.

When I put Greg's *New and Collected Poems* on my desk, the volume opened to a poem titled "Gathering the Bones Together." I remember that poem. Actually, it's quite impossible to forget.

In it Greg tells the story of going hunting with his father and his brothers. As the Orr male coterie, laughing and jostling and chattering together, ran down a slope, Greg accidentally pulled the trigger on his rifle. His brother Peter, age nine, fell to the ground. The poem ends with these lines:

I was twelve when I killed him;
I felt my own bones wrench from my body.
Now I ... walk
beside this river, looking for them.
They have become a bridge
that arches toward the other shore.

That poem sent me looking for other, less sad, ones. I turned to "Making Beasts," a poem I first read almost thirty years ago. I liked it then. I still do.

When I was about 10
I glued together an old
white turtle shell
a woodchuck's skull
and a red squirrel tail
to make my first
mythical beast.

What has been created
is never lost. It crawls
up through my thoughts now
on feet I never gave it.

I thumbed through the book and found the lines I actually had been looking for—what I remembered as "The Dandelion Poem"—what actually is titled "For My Daughter," and begins:

This morning holds intact the skeletal
radiance of a dandelion's globe
bones of delight, a light wind
blows apart.

This summer my older daughter Jo will turn sixteen. She'll take a two-week bicycle trip through Vermont, play in a girls' lacrosse tournament in Maryland, and then teach horseback riding to kids with developmental disabilities. In only two more years, she'll leave for college, a mundane fact I am working hard to accept, but which in truth I actually can't quite fathom.

Trying, that morning, to wrap my mind around this future fact reminded me of the December day in 1967 during winter vacation, when the mailman delivered a thin envelope with a return address of the Admissions Office at Antioch College. I asked my mother if she'd stay there while I opened it and remember her crying as I read her my early acceptance letter. She told me how proud she was of me and that she hoped that my time at Antioch would give me what her years at Bennington had given her—a chance to explore, a place to create, to paint, dance, write poems, to be alive.

The morning I reread Greg's poems, I went outside and picked the remaining dandelions and put them in a canning jar that I filled with water. When my wife Dale saw the jar with the dandelions on the kitchen windowsill, she pointed out that, even in water, weeds wouldn't last long. I replied that I knew dandelions had a reputation for being weeds, but I didn't agree with that when I was nine years old, and forty years later, pretty much, still don't. I then put a Post-It on the page with "For My Daughter" and returned Greg's poetry to the bookshelf within easy reach of my desk.

June 1999

AT INDEPENDENCE PASS

"Things have changed since I first got here." Jo, our seventeen-year-old daughter, was speaking to us from the back seat as she and Dale and I drove through Independence Pass on Colorado State Route 82 this past October.

Independence Pass has an elevation of 12,095 feet. Despite our black sunglasses, the brightness of the reflection of the sun off the snow-covered peaks forced us to squint and look away. But we couldn't take our eyes off the mountains for long.

Dale and I had traveled to Colorado for Parents Weekend at the High Mountain Institute (HMI), which is located outside Leadville, near the foot of Mount Massive. Jo has spent the fall semester there.

At HMI, twenty-five high school juniors devote themselves to a semester with the Rocky Mountains as their science laboratory, astronomy observatory, and artistic inspiration. Although the main building has running water and electricity, the cabins where the kids live have neither. The students split logs for the woodstoves. They cook the meals and clean the buildings as well.

That weekend we parents went to classes. Jo's English class was delving into the mystical environmental poems of Gary Snyder. After sitting in, I wanted to take the course. Her French teacher led a discussion entirely in that language about an existential novel by Sartre. The American history class performed a lengthy analysis of a bicentennial-themed filmstrip—in rap rhythms.

Science class also made an impression. The students, having measured the height and canopy of lodgepole pines with an inclinometer and plotted the results, proved a null hypothesis regarding the relationship between the height of trees and the density of a stand.

We also attended her ethics class. I love the idea that high school kids are required to take an ethics course. It's called "Principles and Practices of the Natural World."

In one of her first letters home, Jo wrote that she had "…an incredible amount of work to do [that] weekend. But you know what? It's not busy work. It all actually means something…." But life and classes at the Institute, while essential to the program, are not the heart of it. Weeks in the wilderness are.

During the semester the students take four backpacking expeditions of ten to twelve days each. On the initial one, in the Sawatch Mountains, they learned to read topographical maps, build a camp, stay relatively safe, and, in the end, leave no trace of their sojourn there. From the photographs Jo sent home, it appeared that in the Sawatches her group had hiked to the top of the world.

On their second excursion, a service trip, the kids built trails and culverts along the Frying Pan River for the Aspen Ranger District. Jo's letter reported that hours of digging dirt and removing rocks was "the hardest and most manual labor that I've ever done, but," she added, "it was great to see our work finished at the end of the day."

That same letter told us that one afternoon her group had been "traversing a boulder field" when [lightning] "began lighting up the sky and hail the size of peas began bouncing off us," so they rushed over huge slabs of rock and "booked down the field." "It was," she continued, "scary but so cool, and what an adrenaline rush!"

In early November, the kids backpacked through the 300-million-year-old, geologically-storied canyons of Utah, with their burnt sienna and copper-colored cliffs and striations of sandstone, limestone, gypsum, and shale. Among other discoveries, they came upon Anasazi pictographs. By then, they all had learned a lot about the West, about depending on themselves and each other, about surviving on the equipment and supplies they were carrying on their backs.

Soon they will begin their final HMI wilderness journey. They'll make their way through the Mosquito Mountains on telemark skis. At night they will sleep in the igloos or quinzhees they will build. They'll study in them, too. The academic courses continue while they're in the wilderness.

In the backcountry, Jo has been trekking with a fifty-five-pound pack—a fact I had heard but not actually appreciated until the Friday of Parents Weekend, when we gave her a big hug hello. Her shoulders felt like bricks. Almost two months had passed since we'd put her on a plane to Denver.

"So how have things changed?" Dale asked, catching a glimpse of Jo in the rearview mirror.

Jo pointed toward Star Mountain and said, "When I first got here, I'd look at a mountain like that and think, 'Wow, how beautiful!' Well, I still think it's beautiful. It's just that now my first thought isn't that. It's 'How long would it take to climb it?'"

December 1999

RADIO WARS

By Leah Newman

Generation gap. To me this phrase means parents are just too old to understand anything. They don't know how to talk or dress, and they have no clue as to what music is currently hot.

CDs are fine to listen to when I'm at home, but my parents, who talk about phonographs and records, can't seem to understand that a CD can actually go in a car. Therefore, when I get into the car, I have no choice but to turn on the radio.

So far, you might be thinking to yourself that this column is going nowhere. Who cares about the radio? Well, I do, and my dad does, too, so that when we get into the car, a problem with the radio arises.

Now, I'm sure many other people also face this predicament, and for my father and me, it's an issue, a problem—what parents sometimes call "a challenge," but maybe it's only my parents who use a word like "challenge." Turning on the radio in the car is usually followed by a discussion with slightly raised, sometimes whiney, occasionally obnoxious voices. By doing this, we avoid an argument.

The only radio station we agree on is an oldies station from Connecticut. I like oldies, but my father's terrible voice trying (well, barely trying) to sing along with Elvis and the Beatles can get just a little annoying. It's not that I don't like the Beatles, and Elvis isn't awful either. It really is my father's voice. If you have ever heard my dad "sing," you know what I'm talking about, and if you haven't, you're lucky.

Bill's other favorite station is [the local NPR station] WFCR. Fresh Air, Car Talk, and All Things Considered with Robert Siegel and Linda Wertheimer aren't exactly my idea of entertainment. And why is the time always something like nineteen minutes past the hour? Why not wait and say twenty minutes? And what's up with "past the hour?" Can't those people just tell us the time?!

Dad hates rap, even rap with a chorus, or rap without any profanity, like Will Smith. He's also not crazy about hip-hop, alternative, or any other music I listen to. Maybe that's a little harsh. He doesn't mind *some* of "my music," but not much. My mother, on the other hand, is in love with Ricky Martin. Dad and I don't always fight in the car. Sometimes the car ride is short enough to skip the radio, but not very often.

My father over the years has somehow turned into my grandfather mixed with some of my granny, and is just starting to realize this. I don't think this realization makes him happy. As much as I love my parents, I have no intention of turning out like them, and so my children will listen to their music in the car, and I will enjoy it.

* * *

By Bill Newman

On a recent school day, my daughter Leah dashed out the front door of the JFK Middle School after her student council meeting, dumped her backpack on the back seat, and hopped into the front. Almost as a reflex, her fingers darted toward the radio selection buttons, but then her fingers, poised to push the buttons, suddenly stopped.

WFCR talking heads were not coming through the speakers. Rather, the Hartford oldies station was playing Aretha Franklin. She glanced over with a look of approval.

Then, to make things even better, we had a chat. After the song had ended, as we sat at the stoplight across from Cooley Dickinson Hospital, Leah asked, "What did you do for oldies when you were a kid?"

I responded with a story. My father walked into my room one evening while my older brother and I were playing "Rock and Roll Is Here to Stay" by Danny and the Juniors. We had just gotten a spindle that allowed us to stack 45-rpm records, so we no longer had to put them on the record player one at a time. My dad announced that the title of the song proved that "this whole rock 'n' roll thing is dying. Otherwise, they wouldn't need a song with words like that." It was 1958.

"And your point?" Leah asked.

Oh yes, the point.

The baby-boomer generation was alive for the birth of rock 'n' roll. This fact, in a word, makes us old or, in two words, at least from our kids' perspective, really old.

OK. So we didn't have oldies. But every year we'd be treated to great new music—from Elvis, Buddy Holly, and Chuck Berry, to the Beatles and the Rolling Stones, Dylan, Donovan and Joan Baez, the Doors, the Who, and the Grateful Dead, Country Joe and the Fish, Frank Zappa and the Mothers of Invention. This list could go on virtually forever—at least up until 1974 or so when my record collection, now replaced in part by tapes and CDs, pretty much ends.

Sometimes, I find that after my kids have commandeered the car radio, certain words have surreptitiously snuck onto my vocal chords, comments like, "Music, you call that music?" Or, "Is that noise really necessary?" Or "It's too loud," or "Turn it down," or "It's giving me a headache." I remember my parents, for whom music has always meant Bing Crosby, Frank Sinatra, and the Andrew Sisters, saying these things.

I loved 1950s and 1960s rock 'n' roll at that time, and I think I was right to insist, when my parents were driving, that we should play it on the car radio. Thirty or forty years later, I still think I'm right. If only National Public Radio would institute an oldies hour, life would be close to perfect.

February 2000

THE RELAY

Our daughters' friend Melissa, then seventeen, was standing at her goalie position on the girls' field hockey team one hot morning when she experienced what she describes as "horrible cramping so bad I couldn't move."

For the next two months Melissa went to doctors but received no definite diagnosis. Her mother Cynthia, a nurse's aid at Sunbridge Nursing Home, wasn't satisfied. After she pressed the gastroenterologist for an ultrasound, he ordered one.

In late October, Melissa skipped her third-period English class and went to Cooley Dickinson Hospital for the test. At home after school, she found her mother on the phone with a doctor. The ultrasound, the doctor reported, had revealed a mass on Melissa's right kidney. That afternoon, while being admitted to the pediatric oncology unit, she asked the doctor, "Can I die from whatever it is?" The doctor replied that he didn't "know *for sure* what the growth was," a technically accurate answer. The following Tuesday a surgical team of seven doctors and staff operated for eight hours to remove Melissa's kidney and the Wilms tumor that had grown inside it.

A Wilms tumor, a fast-growing form of cancer, most often afflicts young children; it's rarely found in teenagers. If the tumor is encapsulated, the odds of survival are good. If cancer cells have escaped from the kidney, it's probably fatal.

When Melissa awakened from the surgery, she looked up at her family standing by her hospital bed. Her dad, she says, "was crying the hardest." Her mother, as Melissa puts it, "had tears, but thought she had to hold everyone together."

Whispering through the oxygen mask, Melissa asked her mother, "It's cancer, isn't it?" And her mother responded, "Yes, but it's a good kind of cancer."

When she emerged from a morphine haze four days later, Melissa learned that she faced more surgery. The doctors needed to insert a portacatheter under her skin near her breastbone to allow chemotherapy to be injected into her bloodstream.

The treatments would last for five months and make most of her hair fall out. She cut the little that remained really short and wore a scarf. She felt fatigued and nauseated all the time, and she once vomited for fourteen straight hours and had to be hospitalized again.

On April 6, 2000—Melissa remembers the date exactly—the doctors removed the portacatheter. Within a week, she says, she was "back to feeling myself except for having no hair."

This spring Melissa will graduate from high school and next fall will start at the University of Massachusetts, Amherst. At the moment she also is working as the honorary co-chairperson of the Hampshire County Relay for Life, sponsored by the American Cancer Society and the Cancer Care Program at our local hospital.

The relay here will begin, as it always does, with the Survivors' Lap. Melissa will be walking with one hundred men, women, and children who share that special bond. When I asked her if she would be walking mostly for the people she knows who are confronting cancer, I expected her to say yes. But she didn't. She told me, instead, that while she of course was walking for friends living with the disease, she was walking just as much for people she didn't know. I must have given her a quizzical look. "Because," she quickly added, "some time in the past, people I didn't know walked for me."

May 2001

LEAVING LEAH: Our Trip to the Inside Passage

"You are about to embark on an adventure, a journey."

On a late afternoon this past August, Dale, Leah and I were sitting together on a knoll at Pitzer College listening to the college president, Laura Trombley. Trombley, who looks at least a decade too young to be a college president, was standing at a portable podium, with the faculty, informally dressed, seated in white folding chairs behind her.

"This four-year enterprise of a liberal arts education," Trombley continued, rarely glancing at her notes and seeming to speak to each student individually, "will cause you to work and think and question. During the next four years, you will make friendships that will last a lifetime and come to know professors who will make an indelible mark on your life and intellect. In this venture, Pitzer College will encourage you to travel widely, but at times you will need to"—she paused to emphasize the next three words—"simply sit still."

She turned to the professors behind her—to her left and then to her right—and said that the time had come for the journey to begin. She asked the faculty to stand and the 220 students of the Pitzer College class of 2008 to leave their seats and their parents and step forward to meet their faculty.

Leah stood up and, along with the rest of her class, walked down the grassy mound toward the professors. My throat felt too tight to make words come out, but Dale managed to whisper to me that she was vowing not to cry until we were safely on the freeway.

At the president's reception that followed, over chicken wings and cut vegetables and with no students in attendance, we spoke with other parents who, like us, were impressed with the consortium of colleges of which Pitzer is a part, called The Claremont Colleges. Located thirty miles east of Los Angeles, the five campuses are intertwined within twelve square blocks. The consortium includes Pomona (the bookstore sells a bumper sticker in Harvard's crimson-and-white colors that says "Harvard: The Pomona of the East"); Scripps, a smart, liberal women's college; Harvey Mudd, a small MIT; Claremont McKenna, a liberal arts college; and Pitzer, founded in 1963, the youngest, most liberal, and most experimental of the five, not unlike my alma mater, Antioch. The colleges share a library, a medical facility, and a bookstore. Students can take classes at any one of them.

At that gathering, we commiserated with parents who, like us, would no longer have any children at home. Dale told one couple about our plans. After leaving Leah, we were taking a trip, traveling through the Inside Passage in Alaska with my law school roommate, Walter, who lived and practiced law in Alaska for many years, and his wife, June.

Walter and I had traveled to Anchorage in 1974 on an internship from Northeastern University School of Law. When I returned to Massachusetts, Walter stayed in Alaska and came back to Boston only briefly to pick up his diploma. He and June a year or two ago moved to Seattle. When he and I spoke this past summer, he suggested that we travel together to Alaska in the fall.

"Sounds like an amazing trip, a great way to get past no kids being at home," the other mother said.

"We all mourn in our own way," Dale quipped

Two days later Dale, Walter, June, and I flew from Seattle to Juneau— over mountains half-hooded in clouds that looked like prehistoric beasts rising out of the sea. I was struck again, as I had been thirty years ago, by an immutable fact about Alaska. Everything is big—almost incomprehensibly big. The Juneau Ice Field equals the size of Rhode Island; Glacier Bay National Park covers about as much acreage as Connecticut; and the Commonwealth of Massachusetts would fit neatly into Denali National Park. If Alaska were cut in half and made into two states, Texas would be the third largest.

Juneau, the state capital, with a population just a little larger than that of my home town, Northampton, Massachusetts, is sandwiched on a slice of land between the Gastineau Channel and the coastal mountains, about halfway through the Inside Passage. The Inside Passage is a ribbon of straits and sounds, channels and passages, islands and inlets that stretches almost 1000 miles from Prince of Wales Island in the south to Glacier Bay and Prince William Sound in the north. The islands protect the passage from the Pacific's leeward winds to its west. The pristine mountains on its eastern shore protect it from the storms of western Canada. The passage, itself mostly wilderness, for centuries has provided a path for explorers.

We flew to Juneau because it is one of the few towns in Southeast Alaska that can be reached by commercial plane. Most are accessible only by boat or small plane, and none can be reached by car because no roads connect any towns in what Alaskans call "Southeast."

Within an hour of our plane landing, June, Walter, Dale, and I were hiking on Perseverance Path, heading toward Mount Juneau. After only ten minutes on the trail, we found ourselves in a lush rain forest of Sitka spruce, northern hemlock, mountain ash, devil's club ferns, berry bushes, and streams and waterfalls hidden from the town below by the canopy of the forest. As we walked, the peaks, with their year-round snow, came into view. Though many miles away, the immensity of the mountains made them appear almost close enough to touch.

We hiked for about six hours, four up and two down. Away from the streams and waterfalls, the forest was silent and streaked with light. We felt far away from everyone and everything except each other.

We talked about many things but blessedly little about law. Walter for years had been a superb appellate attorney. One of his briefs to the Alaska Supreme Court in a criminal case began, "It was a dark and stormy night," followed by appropriate citations to the record. At oral argument the justices applauded his statement of the facts, particularly that first sentence. The result? Walter won. But Walter doesn't practice law any more.

In law school, when Walter and I shared an apartment, first on Beacon Street in Boston and later in Anchorage, he watercolored a lot, and he has become an accomplished watercolorist, painting landscapes, seascapes, and cityscapes. He transforms those paintings into prints and cards. A few years ago he closed his law office to become a full-time artist. His prints, cards, and desk calendars are found in galleries and gift shops in Alaska, Washington, and Oregon. Last year he sold over 60,000 cards through the business he calls WalterColors.

During our hike Walter, who lived in Juneau when he was a public defender, explained that the more than 100 inches of yearly rainfall creates the lushness of the forest. When I expressed amazement at 100 inches of rain, Walter added that in some parts of Southeast, yearly rain fall averages 350 to 400 inches.

The next day we four hiked a trail alongside the Mendenhall Glacier. The Mendenhall, Juneau's most famous glacier, is one of 100,000 in Alaska, most of them unnamed.

Think of a glacier as a river—a river of ice. It moves slowly, less than half a mile a year. Glaciers can be thousands of feet deep and many miles long. Some, although not all, are fed by ice fields, which are, in essence, massive frozen lakes. Ice fields don't move, but they do overflow their banks and feed glaciers. On the ice field above the glaciers in Juneau, which stretches 120 miles north into British Columbia, it snows more than 100 feet each year.

That afternoon, every time we came to a clearing or an opening where we could see the Mendenhall, I felt as if we were looking at it for the first time. My mind just couldn't retain the brightness and enormity of the glacier. And although thousands of people must have hiked this trail, that afternoon, with no one else on it, it felt as if it had been created only for us.

In the evening we had dinner with friends of Walter and June's. We sat on their deck and watched the sun set in panoramic pinks, oranges, and reds over Auke Bay and the Chilkat Range. The colors in Alaska are as intense as the sizes and distances are massive.

The sun was shining again the next morning when we took a helicopter to the Gilkey Glacier, about thirty-five miles northeast of the city at the edge of a massive ice field. Already equipped by Alaska Northstar Expeditions with insulated clothing, boots, and helmets, after hopping off the helicopters we were handed crampons and ice picks as well.

Our guides, two men and two women, spoke excitedly about coming to this glacier. Because it takes perfect weather for helicopters to fly here, they explained, they could visit the Gilkey only two or three times a summer, which is also to say, two or three times a year. They were returning to the glacier after a hiatus of five or six weeks.

Our guides explained that the brilliant hue of the ice all around us—intense cerulean, turquoise, aquamarine—was caused by the ice being so compressed that it filters out all the other colors of the spectrum. Next they pointed out the medial moraine, a phenomenon that looks like tire tracks on pristine snow made by gigantic tanks that had first driven through a tar and gravel pit. A moraine is rows of rocks and sand forced to the surface when glaciers collide.

Then they spoke about the icefalls cascading above us. My eyes were staring at those ice falls, but again my mind was having a hard time accepting that what I was seeing was real. The icefalls looked like chiseled, sculpted, clear-and-white glass thousands of feet tall. My mind had barely enough space to hear that an icefall is a glacier's version of a waterfall.

Next, with our crampons crunching the ice, we followed our guides across the glacier to the edge of crevasses hundreds of feet deep. They invited us to gaze into them but, please, don't fall in because if you do you'll end up wedged, unable to move, in an icy vise grip with virtually no chance of being rescued, they said. But do take a moment, they next suggested, to stand still and listen to absolute silence. We did. We listened to absolute silence suddenly broken by, "A moulin! A moulin!"

The guides almost simultaneously had spotted a newly formed ice cave, called a moulin. Beware of twenty-somethings in great physical condition who grew up mountaineering and need to take you with them so they can go exploring, I told myself. The thought of entering an unexplored ice cave made me feel more than a little claustrophobic, but I was urged on by a thought I often had on this trip—that I probably would never again have the chance to do this. We all followed them inside the moulin.

By our third day in Juneau we had rather cavalierly exited a rain forest after dark, after being lost, paid no mind that our helicopter appeared to be flying into a mountain peak, and dismissed the possibility of falling into a 200-foot crevasse. But after returning from Gilkey Glacier, Dale and I found ourselves confronted with a dilemma that actually did disturb us, a question without a clear answer: Should we call Leah?

As the author Anne Lamott points out, kids, unfortunately, don't come with operating instructions. And while we hope to improve at parenting as our kids grow older, that hope mostly exhibits the fallacy that experience somehow brings wisdom. To me, parenting forever feels like driving while looking in the rearview mirror.

We missed Leah and wanted to call her. But a call from us might make her think that we were acting like over-anxious parents and not treating her as an adult. On the other hand, if we didn't call, she might worry that something had happened to us, or maybe we weren't as caring and loving as we professed to be.

After much discussion, we decided that we'd given this question more than sufficient consideration, searched for a location with some cell phone service, and called. Leah was happy to hear from us. In fact, she seemed a tad miffed that we hadn't called sooner.

She talked nonstop for ten minutes. She and her roommate were becoming fast friends. They hadn't finished decorating their room, but it was coming along. Pitzer definitely was the best of the five colleges. She liked the kids in her dormitory and two professors in particular. One professor acted a bit eccentric but, she thought, entertainingly eccentric. She had played Ultimate Frisbee. Were we having a good time? Any adventures? Great! And thanks for the postcard and our news, but she needed to finish a paper and had to go.

The next day we took a boat trip, leaving Juneau on Stephen's Passage on our way to Tracy Arm, a fjord, which the captain, Steve, explained is a body of water with only one entrance and one exit.

"Walter, I need a remedial lesson," I said quietly enough for no one else to hear.

"Shoot."

"If a fjord has one entrance and exit, and the exit here is completely blocked by a massive tidal glacier—that's our destination by the way—that would mean there is no exit, so how is this going to work?"

"Relax, grasshopper," he told me. "You must listen carefully. One exit that is also the entrance. If you get back to where you started, you're good. I've heard, though, that on this trip that's not as easy as it sounds, that sometimes boats get stuck in the ice. By the way, do you remember how Sartre's *No Exit* turns out?"

"I knew you when you were funny," I told him.

Then perhaps a dozen of us from, as they say in Alaska, The Lower 48, stepped onto the gangplank and walked aboard the *Adventure Bound*.

"Expect icebergs as we get closer to Tracy Arm," Steve announced soon after we embarked, a statement that for me immediately conjured images of the *Titanic*. First I tried to remember if my will was in order but then felt mollified by the color of the water in the fjord, which was, despite the drizzle, a beautiful, Caribbean greenish-blue. Having been to Jamaica, I knew that the sun reflecting off the sand at the bottom creates those amazing shades of turquoise and aquamarine and that such reflection happens only in relatively shallow water. For reasons not totally clear, the water depth being relatively shallow, twenty or thirty feet perhaps, made me feel safer.

Still, alerted to the danger posed by icebergs, I thought I'd mosey over to ask Steve about the depth of the water. He informed me the seafloor was about 1600 feet below us. The greenish-blue color, it turns out, is caused by glacial sediment suspended not far below the surface. He added, in response to another of my nonchalant questions, that the water temperature was about thirty-two degrees Fahrenheit.

After about an hour we indeed began to encounter icebergs. On the surface, some appeared not much bigger than our back deck at home, while others approximated the size of a ranch house. The captain reminded us that eighty-five percent of an iceberg's mass remains underneath the water. Icebergs, Steve explained, are created by calving, the term for chunks of ice breaking off the face of the glacier into the water below. We'd probably see calving. With a little luck, he added, not too close to the *Adventure Bound*.

The captain throttled down the engine as we approached an iceberg that had split in two in front of the boat seconds earlier. The first section was about forty feet high. The second, having a changed center of gravity, was rolling over, causing waves to smash against the bow. The split in the iceberg revealed the brilliant blue of its interior. The captain's voice exuded excitement. "You just don't get to see this every day," he announced over the small PA system. "You really don't."

A few minutes later Steve's voice was coming over the PA again. He wanted to share with us information about "shooters." Some icebergs, he explained, calve below the surface and travel submerged for some distance before shooting out of the water with enormous velocity. Sometimes the iceberg rushing toward the surface smashes into an iceberg above it, causing the one nearer the surface to shoot up out of the water.

I returned to the stern to gaze again at the mountainous blue iceberg rolling topsy turvy a few feet off the starboard side. I felt better about our present predicament. After all, why bother worrying about that iceberg rolling over and capsizing us when at any moment a shooter the size of a small mountain might smash through the hull of our boat?

As we continued drawing closer to South Sawyer Glacier, at the opposite end of the fjord, its appearance struck me as even more improbable than the blues of the icebergs. That glacier looked like a 100-square-mile piece of meringue with brown sugar—actually, surface boulders and crushed rock—sprinkled on top.

Steve maneuvered the last couple hundred yards through ice floes to the glacier. We passed a half dozen seals, each ensconced on its own iceberg, like homeowners in their backyards on a Saturday afternoon. They didn't move, didn't even twitch, at the sight of us.

As we were bobbing near the glacier with the engine cut, the wind came up and pushed together the ice floes and icebergs that now were behind the stern. Looking back, a route to clear water no longer existed.

Walter and I revisited that one entrance, one exit, no exit problem and chatted about the possibility of our imminent participation in a re-creation of the Shackleton expedition. When the time came to leave, the captain, averaging perhaps one or two knots, nudged the boat into icebergs, steered through tiny openings, and after what seemed like hours, had us in open water. Back in Stephen's Passage we encountered 25-ton humpback whales spouting and blowing. One breached not more than fifty yards from our boat. Steve steered around the occasional iceberg.

The following evening, after a hike through the rain and mist and low clouds above Juneau, we caught an overnight ferry, the *Taku*, part of the fleet of the Alaska Marine Highway System, to Sitka.

Sitka, the former capital of Russian America, is a town of less than 9000 on Baronof Island between Whale Bay to the south, Salisbury Sound to the north, and Kruzof Island and Mount Edgecumbe to the west. We really wanted to call Leah from the ferry but found that only ten minutes from Juneau all cell phone service had vanished. Instead, that evening Dale and I wrote her two more postcards and a long note.

The *Taku* was carrying only a few passengers on this—its last—voyage of the season. It sailed so slowly and quietly through the narrow straits, bounded on both sides by the undisturbed and protected Tongass National Forest, it seemed that the boat, like us, did not want to disturb the quiet. There were no ripples on the water, even in the rain.

We arrived in Sitka at about eleven in the morning and by early afternoon were hiking up Gavan Hill. "How could anyone call this mountain a hill?" I asked Dale and Walter a number of times, first seriously and then rhetorically, and then mumbled that question to myself some more, as we ascended over 2000 feet in four hours. Gavan Hill has steps in some locations because without them the trail would frequently become a river in that rain forest. Maybe a mountain can't have steps— that's why it's called a hill, I thought to myself. We kept climbing. Every time it felt like we must be approaching the summit, we'd turn a corner only to see more steps and more trail in front of us.

The next day we took another boat trip—this one around Sitka Sound, where we saw more spouting humpback whales, as well as seals, eagles, puffins, loons, and a rack of otters swimming backward, lying on their backs with their hands resting on their bellies. That afternoon we went kayaking in the sound up to the mouth of the Indian River, where we saw enormous flocks of seagulls and thousands, perhaps tens of thousands, of coho salmon struggling their way upstream to spawn.

After spawning, salmon die, and we saw seagulls blanketing both the sky and shores of the river and feasting on those dead fish. For seagulls, the eyes of the salmon are a delicacy. When we returned later that day to the mouth of the river to see the salmon run some more, we stepped over thousands of dead, eyeless salmon.

That evening we found cell phone service outside a sushi bar and called Leah. Although she had known our plans, she sounded annoyed that we hadn't returned home yet. "You know," she said, "you didn't take trips like that when I was your daughter." Fortunately, she was laughing. "But *seriously*," she went on, "I need some things."

"Like what?"

"Like a batik bedspread from Faces (a 1960s redux retail store in our hometown). "So *when exactly* will you guys be home?"

Yes, yes, yes. Everything was fine, she reported: classes, friends, professors, the dorm, food and—she sounded particularly excited about this—the pool at Scripps was spectacular. (Leah swam competitively in high school.) She was on her way, she told us, to a kickboxing class at Harvey Mudd and then, after dinner at Pomona, needed to finish a novel for her freshman seminar.

Two days later we flew home from Seattle. As we walked through the back door into the kitchen, I was struck by our house's uncharacteristic quiet. I picked up the mail from the front hall and carried it to the kitchen table, but didn't open it. Instead, I telephoned our older daughter, Jo, who was taking a semester off from the Tisch School for the Arts at New York University to live and work in San Francisco. I spoke to her voice mail. Then I called Leah, but again, reached only a recording.

As I sat at the table looking at the images in our digital camera of our recent journey and listening to the kitchen wall clock tick, I reconsidered the wisdom of our decision to skip the hour-long seminar that Pitzer had offered the parents of freshmen on the "empty nest syndrome." I had avoided it in part because I figured it would be taught by a tree hugger trained at Esalen and in part because we'd been otherwise engaged in an important activity—shopping for a refrigerator small enough to tuck away in Leah's dorm room. I mused about how much we'd like to return to Alaska and how happy we'd be to travel almost anywhere with Walter and June, for friendship, too, is an adventure.

But parenting daughters, I thought, also has been an amazing adventure. An adventure? Really? My mind became engaged in a spirited debate with itself.

How about the night we busted Jo for driving when she was too young even to have a learner's permit? Not to mention the times we intruded on her and her girlfriends in the basement, hanging out with those alleged human beings called boys. Or the classes she cut. Or the graduation and other parties with absurd amounts of alcohol. Or, for that matter, at age four or five running away ("to Maine" she later told us) with our dog, Caboose, and her friend, Becky. And how about Leah when she was maybe five, hiding under the deck and hearing me screaming to find her while I frantically searched all over the neighborhood, fearing she was hurt, lost, or kidnapped—just a prank, dad, she later explained. Or her falling off the chairlift when she was eight and our rushing to the emergency room. And the arguments about whether the piles of clothes and books and shoes and plates with a patina of crusted food and un-identifiable detritus of God-knows-what-else in her room constituted a public health hazard. Now there, all that should cut down on the sloppy sentimentality.

"A great adventure?" I asked myself again as I walked to the kitchen counter to boil water for my decaffeinated black tea.

Well, actually—as I poured the hot water from the kettle into a mug—yes.

Leaving Leah and our recent travels brought home to me that parenting daughters for the past twenty-one years has given me the best adventure I'll ever have. That journey has shown me an emotional landscape I didn't know existed. It has made me marvel at our potential to love. It has made me happy.

The time has come, I understand, for new adventures. The problem is, I didn't want the last one to end.

October 2004

MY PARENTS

MINUENDS
IN THE MEADOWS

At six o'clock, the morning of my birthday this year, I found myself sitting up in bed trying to catch a dream, but it escaped.

Downstairs, our golden retriever, Casey, opened one eye and didn't even pretend to feel guilty about sleeping on the couch. "Ball? Stick? Out?" But no words could entice her to move. She took a deep breath and closed her open eye. I was on my own.

With coffee in hand, on dirt roads that have names only on a surveyor's map, I took a walk through the Meadows of Northampton. I had the cornfields, the Connecticut River, and the sun rising over the Holyoke Range to myself. Near the single-lane bridge by the Oxbow, I found myself absentmindedly doing subtraction in my head. The minuend (that's the top number in a subtraction problem, the number being subtracted from) was a possible lifespan, the subtrahend (the number being subtracted) was the age I had turned that day.

$$85 - 47 = 38$$
$$80 - 47 = 33$$
$$70 - 47 = 23$$

I stopped there. I can imagine twenty-three years going by.

On my birthday twenty-three years ago, Richard Nixon announced he was resigning as president. Talk about a great birthday present! I can picture clearly watching his abdication on my first color television. It doesn't feel that long ago to me.

As I ambled back through the kitchen door at about eight o'clock, Casey was barking for breakfast; my daughters were demanding to know where I had been; I was preoccupied with the problems of a murder client; and the phone was ringing. "I didn't wake you, did I?" It was my father. I went to the quiet of my office at home to speak with him.

"So," he said after wishing me a happy birthday, "forty-seven." It was half a question, half a statement.

"Not so old," I responded, recalling the adage to which I had once categorically subscribed: "Never trust anyone over thirty."

But then I added, "But not so young."

"Forty-seven. Sounds pretty good to me," he commented.

My parents are getting older. I try not to think about this fact that rides like a stowaway in my mind.

My father, always politically conservative, considers Ronald Reagan a great president. When I marched in my first antiwar demonstration at age sixteen, he didn't understand it. I still march in political demonstrations, and he still doesn't really understand why.

But some years after the Vietnam War ended, he and I declared peace. After that, we spent long hours sitting in the comfortable armchairs of our disagreements.

My dad planned, after speaking with me, to go swimming and horseback riding and then put in a full day at his office. He doesn't look or act like almost seventy-seven, but he is; and seventy-seven is more than some of the minuends I had just considered in the Meadows. As I put the phone back in its cradle, I glanced up at the best present he has ever given me.

One Sunday about ten years ago, when I was visiting at his home, he asked if there was anything special I wanted him to leave me in his will. I felt awkward but he had asked me a serious question and I responded with a serious answer: the painting that had hung for years on the wall behind his father's desk, that now hung next to his bedroom door. My dad and I then went upstairs, and he took that painting off its hook and handed it to me. "Here," he said, "I'd rather know that you're enjoying it while I'm alive."

The painting, by a little-known, twentieth-century Italian artist, Aldo Affortunati, shows a solitary man leading a large grey Andalusian horse up a country road. He is lightly holding the reins and leaning forward against a wind that is bending the trees, swirling dirt around the horse's hooves, and billowing the orange cape tied to the saddle. Because we see only the man's back, his age is hard to gauge. Despite the instancy of the storm, the man belongs on that road. He is comfortable being on his own journey. That evening I hung that painting on the wall above my desk at my office at home. It has been there ever since.

My father and I see the world through different lenses, which is not surprising, I suppose. The defining events for him were the Great Depression and serving as the navigation officer on a Navy LST (Landing Ship, Tank) in the South Pacific during World War II. The formative ones for me were participating in the upheaval of the 1960s and protesting the war in Vietnam.

That painting brings into focus a less tangible, but more important, legacy. Even though my father had definite views on the way the world should spin on its axis and what causes it to wobble, he gave me the ability and freedom to make my own choices. I don't think this was easy for him to do.

Some day some years from now I may have a conversation with my daughters similar to the one my father and I had before he gave me the Affortunati. I hope that long before then, either I will have passed on to them the same ability and freedom, or they will have claimed that freedom as a birthright. If they do, when for me the minuend and the subtrahend in my morning math problem are equal, the actual number won't matter so much.

September 1997

SEARCHING FOR BLUE SEA GLASS

His birth certificate read Abraham James Gewirtz, and we all called him Jimmy, except my daughters, who called him Grandpa Doc.

I met Jimmy in 1961 when I was eleven years old and at first certainly didn't call him Jimmy.

My mother had taken me to a doctor's office to see a dermatologist, not a word I knew then. Upon examining my foot, the doctor informed us that the wart on the bottom should be removed but that he couldn't perform the procedure that day. I needed another appointment. A week or so later, my mother brought me back to Jimmy's office, whereupon he removed my wart. I screamed a lot, really a lot. (Note to mom: I suppose it's a little late, but I am sorry about that part.) When my mother and I returned to have my post-operative wartless foot examined, it turned out that another wart had popped up. So we repeated the procedure. After about my seventh visit to see him, the wart removals having been accomplished, Jimmy presented me with a present—the warts in a jar.

At home I placed the jar with those warts prominently on my bookshelf. That evening my mother came into my room and from a safe distance peered at my former warts (my mother has always hated snakes and worms and gross things, so—jar or not—she wasn't coming anywhere near them). My parents had been divorced for some years; my father was remarried and I had grown beyond the idea that they might get back together. "Mom," I said, "I don't care how much you and that doctor want to see each other, I'm not gluing the warts back on, and I'm not growing any more. Go on a date, already. Please."

They did. For over forty years they did. Although they never married and kept their own apartments, they were inseparable.

Jimmy grew up in the early part of last century on the Lower East Side of New York, wanting to become a doctor. But his family couldn't begin to pay for college, and at that time medical schools had a quota for Jews that, though rarely discussed, was strictly enforced.

Undeterred, Jimmy worked his way through Long Island University and then taught himself French so he could attend medical school in Quebec, where all the courses were taught in that language. He graduated first in his class at medical school, became an accomplished doctor, and practiced medicine for over sixty years.

Early on a Thursday morning this June, Jimmy, who at ninety-two was handsome and slim, had a full head of white hair, and still thoroughly enjoyed playing golf, watching sports, and reading books, particularly biographies, walked into a New York hospital for an operation. Before the surgery, we believed that he'd be just fine and walk out, but he didn't make it off the operating table.

In August, our daughter Jo, now nineteen, brought with her on our vacation to the beach a collection of pictures of her Grandpa Doc. Some photos show her and her sister, Leah, now sixteen, cooking brownies, with fudge smeared over their faces, with Jimmy looking on bemused. There were recent pictures from Thanksgivings and birthdays and older ones of our girls on Jimmy's lap as he read picture books to them.

Time together, I've learned, can create its own rituals. This year, on late August afternoons, Dale, Jo, Leah, and I would sit on the porch, looking out over the ocean. Sometimes we'd share the photographs Jo had brought. During other twilights we'd sort by color the sea glass we had collected that day.

Although some people call it beach glass, "sea glass" strikes me as more apt and accurate. After all, it's the churning of the glass in the sand by the waves that transforms broken bottles into smooth pieces of almost organic art.

We found an abundance of it on the slice of land we quickly came to consider our beach—many pieces of green glass, and quite a few amber ones, too. Less frequently, we'd find clear pieces, sometimes mottled, sometimes transparent. Rarer still were pieces with a pink hue and those with a beginning-of-sunrise shade of yellow.

Deep blue was the rarest. We could spend an hour or more at low tide under an orange sunset and find only a few pieces of cobalt-colored glass.

Considering sea glass as art does seem a bit oxymoronic. After all, it begins mostly as discarded beer bottles—green for Heineken, brown for Budweiser, clear for Miller. The genesis of the blue probably is something as pedestrian as Noxzema or Milk of Magnesia.

But the origins of sea glass feel irrelevant. Its beginnings do not diminish its sensuousness.

Jo suggested that we arrange the most luminous pieces in a bottle as a gift for my mother, who my daughters call Granny. Jo's idea reminded me how much Jimmy and my mother loved the sea—its tranquility and its variability, too. Jimmy had confided to my mother that upon his death, he wished to be cremated and his ashes spread in New York Harbor, near Ellis Island. This fall my mother will fulfill his wish.

One evening this summer, when Dale and I and our girls were sitting on the beach reminiscing about Jimmy, Leah and I talked about our research for the eulogy I gave at the celebration of his life. My original draft had ended with the word "amen," but I realized I didn't really understand the meaning of the word or know its etymology. Leah volunteered to accompany me to the library to find out.

Amen, we discovered, has roots in Latin, French, and Greek as well as Hebrew. In Talmudic times, responding "amen" was the main form of participation in a religious service, not only because congregations were unfamiliar with the prayer texts, but also because public worship mainly took the form of one person speaking and the rest responding. Saying "amen" was viewed as equivalent to reciting the blessing itself. Over time, "amen" has been used as a noun, synonymous with certainty or truth; as a verb meaning to strengthen or confirm; as an adverb equivalent to surely; and as an interjection, translated as "so be it," "it is true," or "may it become true." "Amen" has also been interpreted as an expression of hope.

As the sun set, the ocean was still. So were we. We were sad thinking about Jimmy. As the horizon filled with a pink afterglow, Leah said, "Amen."

From our week together this summer, the memory that will remain with me the most is our walks on the beach at sunset. On our last walk, while we searched for more blue sea glass to put in our collection for Granny, I was thinking about my last conversation with Jimmy the night before he went to the hospital. When we spoke, we mostly commiserated about the New York Jets. I'd give a lot to be able to do that telephone call over so that at least once in my life I would have told him that I loved him.

June 2002

A SUNDAY ON THE STAIRS

The day was quiet, as Sundays often are, although it might have been a Saturday, I suppose. In my memory, the photograph of that day more than fifty years ago was taken through an amber filter that softens the meadows and hills and melds their colors, making them thick and rich, like finger paints. I must have been seven, not yet eight, because it was before the divorce. We were all still living together in the house on Highland Road in Harrison, New York.

We were visiting my grandmother, my mother's mother, who lived near the town limits of Katonah. Hers was a New England postcard house, with white clapboards and black shutters. The house had no yard because she lived in the country and needed no fences. The suburbs where we lived weren't like that.

As soon as our dad stopped the car, my brother, sister, and I jumped out and raced to the front door because the winner—this was the prize—could make the doorbell chime. Our grandmother opened the door immediately after my brother pushed the bell. Then she hugged us in descending order of our ages, my brother first, then me, then our sister. Then she let me and my sister push the doorbell too, and then she let my brother make the bells chime yet again. After all, he had won the race fair and square, more or less.

Later that morning I was holding a glass of water in my hand, a tall glass, which meant it would have come from a kitchen cabinet. I don't remember any adult handing it to me; my brother and sister and I all were too short to reach the cabinet; and none of us, I'm pretty sure, would have dared to stand on a chair or crawl up on a counter to reach the cupboard in my grandmother's kitchen.

I do remember taking a sip as I started down the stairs that led to where the backyard would have been if she'd had one. The railing was on my right, and I was holding the glass in my right hand. I have no memory why I would have been going outside with a glass of water or why I didn't switch it to my left hand and hold onto the railing.

I also have no memory of slipping or tripping and I can't conjure the sensation of falling, but if I close my eyes and concentrate on that moment, I can still hear the sound of glass being crushed on the concrete stairs, when my head landed on it. I do remember lying on my side with my knees curled against my chest, my left foot resting on a riser, the top of my head pushing against the screen door, and blood running off my neck, pooling underneath my ear. And my mother's voice yelling my father's name.

My father wouldn't have driven alone to rush to find help. Logic tells me that I was in the back seat lying on my mother's lap—although, in truth, I can't recall if I was lying or sitting, or in the front seat or the back. I'm pretty sure that most of the time my eyes were closed and that I felt sick to my stomach, that blood was seeping through the towel pressed to my head and that I heard a voice say we didn't have time to drive to the hospital. At some point my father lifted me out of the car and ran up some stairs carrying me. If forced to say, I would describe the stairs as wooden and the hallway as dark, but I really don't know if this is true. I do remember my father cradling me, my head in the warm, sticky towel on his arm, and I still can hear the sound of his fist banging on the doctor's door that would not open.

After that, it's hard to get the sequence straight. I can see colors, but no clear images. I can conjure the sense of lying on a hard table under a hot, bright light that poured through my eyelids and turned the black to pink. I think I knew I was in a hospital. I could sense people standing over me. Once again, there was no time for something, a word I did not know, the something there was no time for.

I felt cords being strapped around my ankles and a belt being cinched across my waist and leather straps tying down both my wrists. Then, with no anesthesia, the word I did not know, a doctor poured iodine into the seven-inch gash that began at my right temple.

It felt as if a hot poker had been inserted into my brain, and I remember screaming and with all my strength trying to rip my hands and feet out of the restraints as the doctors began to pull out shards of glass. But I also remember my dad's calm voice saying that I should squeeze his hand as hard as I could, and I remember squeezing his hand with all my might, and I remember him telling me that it would be all right, and to this day I remember believing him.

For my father's funeral
April 2006

AND MY
GRANDPARENTS

GRANDPA'S DOOR

My grandfather's favorite joke when I was a kid: "When is a door not a door?" Answer: "When it's ajar."

Grandpa would laugh and I would grin, feeling both befuddled and too embarrassed to admit I didn't get it. How could a door become a jar? I was lost.

In my memory grandpa told me this joke about a million times. Finally, one day, at long last, my dad, overhearing his father being unable to resist asking "When is a door..." and seeing me respond—or not—blessedly took me aside and explained the riddle.

Ajar is now back in my life, thanks to our acquisition of a Dodge Caravan. Among the myriad data and messages displayed on the dashboard appear the words "Door Ajar."

"Door Open" would have done fine. Because "Door Ajar" lights up when a door is open completely as well as when one is not slammed tight, "ajar" not only is too fancy a word, it's the wrong one, at least some of the time. In addition, "Door Ajar" has engendered a predictable refrain from our daughters, "No, dad, please, we'll slam the door—anything but that stupid joke again."

The seismic jolt that the Caravan's "ajar" causes to my linguistic tranquility is mild, however, compared to another one of the car's electronic mindbenders, which says, "Check Gages." Say what? Check what? "G-A-G-E-S?"

As a consumer I'd feel better if Chrysler could spell "gauge." After all, if the folks who designed the engine relate to mechanical things as well as the "gage" guy does to English, Chrysler could be guaranteeing us a very long seven years or 70,000 miles.

Of course, corporations have a long history of mangling English. Around the time my grandfather was inflicting "ajar" on me, the R.J. Reynolds Tobacco Company was searing into my memory the jingle, "Winston tastes good like a cigarette should."

Accept for a moment that a cigarette can taste good and forget that this slogan results in people contracting emphysema and dying of cancer. Now recall the early grammar lessons that "like," used appropriately, governs a noun or a pronoun, e.g., "Cigarettes, like guns, cause death." "Like" may not substitute for "as" before a phrase or clause. Properly stated, the slogan should read, "Winston tastes good AS a cigarette should."

Nonetheless, by repeating millions of times "like a cigarette should"—an addictive phrase, fitting for its addictive product—Winston not only has killed a lot of people, but it also has contributed to the death of good English.

I used to like "like"—a useful word, usually a verb, connoting something positive but less intense than passion, as in, "I like hamburgers but love chocolate." "Like" is also properly a preposition. For example, the sentence in the previous paragraph comparing guns and cigarettes worked like a charm.

Today, however, "like" is so omnipresent in my daughters' conversations, I have no idea what part of speech it is.

Consider for example, the run-on sentence "We went to Bart's for ice cream, like everybody was there." In that sentence "like" could be a conjunction substituting for "and" (and everyone was there), or it could be an adjective meaning "almost," modifying everyone (almost everyone was there), or an adverb modifying the verb was (everyone was really there).

Of course, "like" often substitutes for the interjection "well," as in "Like, how are you." And because neither an adjective nor an adverb can modify an interjection such as "Wow!" the phrase "Like wow!" doesn't actually exist in English, except it does all the time.

No doubt there will be an entire generation who, raised believing, or at least accepting, that "like" is an all-purpose adverb, conjunction, interjection, and preposition, will also believe that a gage gives information. Gage is, to be sure, a fine English word, but a gage (as in "throwing down a gage," which means giving a pledge or presenting a challenge) doesn't have anything to do with gauging the infirmity of a mechanical part.

I know, I know. I'm being picky and old fashioned. English evolves. Usages change. Sometimes "like" merely is substituting for umms and ahhs.

Worse than that, I've probably been deluding myself in even entertaining the possibility that corporate advertising execs might care about their lousing up English. After all, why would multinational corporations treat the language with any more respect than they treat their employees, communities, and the environment? Like someday they won't make billions on weapons and war.

August 1994

AND HIS FRIGATES

When I was seven or eight, maybe nine, I carefully would paste a book-plate inside the front cover of my books. The bookplate, an etching of a square-rigger, showed these words of Emily Dickinson underneath the ship: *There is no frigate like a book to take us lands away.*

This August, when my wife Dale, Jo, Leah, and I went to Cape Cod for vacation, I brought with me the books that had been accumulating on my nightstand: *High Tide in Tucson* by Barbara Kingsolver; *Traveling Mercies: Some Thoughts on Faith* by Anne Lamott; *Home and Away* by National Public Radio host Scott Simon; and *Close Range—Wyoming Stories* by Annie Proulx. With a lot of luck I'd have time to read the books I brought with me. The last thing I needed was another one.

Still, a day or two after we arrived, while meandering down Commercial Street in Provincetown, I found myself in a small bookstore. There I happened upon a book by Paul Schneider, the son of western Massachusetts poet and author Pat Schneider. When I opened *The Enduring Shore: A History of Cape Cod, Martha's Vineyard, and Nantucket*, the opening passage about a Wampanoag Indian, Epenow, who had been enslaved by the English in 1611 but later escaped, caught my eye:

> *How many times had he thought about the last lobster*
> *he had eaten, the last clambake on the beach before a*
> *warm fire, the sloppy hands and cool air. How many*
> *times had he wondered when, or if ever, such perfect*
> *days would come again?*

I bought the book.

Perhaps a half hour later, I had walked up the 116 stairs and sixty ramps to the top of Pilgrim Monument. There the reflection of the late afternoon sun on Provincetown Harbor looked like ribbons of sequins. Fishing boats, as well as dinghies and dories, many small sailboats, and one impressive, sleek white schooner were bobbing at their moorings. There was brine—you could taste it—in the air. It was easy to imagine sailors on tall ships casting off from the Cape.

I would guess that the view conjured my memory of the bookplates. I'd been musing about my grandfather on that day, the anniversary of his death. A prodigious and prolific reader and an inveterate traveler, too, he had given me those bookplates as a gift.

As I squinted toward the ocean, I recalled finding him in 1969 in Venice, Italy. I'd been bumming around Europe that summer, full of self-pity after Wendy had broken up with me, carrying one thing of value—a Eurail Pass, which gave me unlimited train travel. Many late evenings I would go to a station—in Amsterdam, Brussels, or Geneva—and board any train scheduled for a run of eight hours of more. Sleeping on a train saved the cost of a youth hostel.

This way of seeing the world worked well for a while. It included a mesmerizing ride to the Arctic Circle and the midnight sun. After a night on the deck of a trawler through the fjords of Norway, I caught a train south to Oslo, then on to Copenhagen and, later, Vienna.

But distances in western Europe are relatively short, and I was running out of eight-hour train rides, which is why I boarded the overnight to Venice. On the way there, I vaguely recalled that my grandfather and his wife, Liz, had planned to travel to Venice that summer, perhaps around that date. After I arrived, I checked a number of hotels and to my surprise—by serendipity—found them.

Grandpa was seventy-three and very Republican. I was nineteen and, if given the chance, would have voted for a presidential ticket of Bob Dylan and Allen Ginsberg. Grandpa and Liz were staying at a fancy hotel. I found a bunk at a youth hostel.

At dinner that night Grandpa said to me, "Always travel when you can. You never know if the chance will come again." At the time, I thought he was merely dispensing advice. In retrospect, I think, he wanted me to see that we shared common ground. After all, although we were living in different worlds, so to speak, we also were contentedly sitting together in Piazza San Marco.

Without traffic, it only takes two-and-a-half hours to drive from Northampton to the Bourne or the Sagamore bridge, both of which span the Cape Cod Canal and connect that isthmus to the rest of Massachusetts. Not a long trip, but the ocean, the clam shacks, the National Seashore, and the sunsets make me feel as if I've traveled quite far.

And, after arriving there, I traveled further. Books this summer have taken me to the Bay Area with Anne Lamott; given me a tour of Chicago with Scott Simon; showed me extraordinary vistas of Arizona through the eyes of Barbara Kingsolver; allowed me to tour Wyoming with Annie Proulx; and sailed me along the shores and islands of Massachusetts and to ports around the world with Paul Schneider. Those trips gave me back the feeling many of us first know as children, the joy of loving books.

My father's father was a voracious reader, who wanted me to read less pulp fiction and more Shakespeare. My mother's mother—we called her G.G.—also loved books and taught me to read when I was very young. She'd sit with me on the two-seater couch in the den and help me sound out the words of the Bufferin ads in *Life* magazine. My grandmother, no doubt, would have approved of my journeying with these pages and words and authors this summer. My grandfather would have, too. When I became an adult, my grandparents and I would often ask each other, early in a conversation, "What are you reading?" All of us always had an answer.

I love the tactile sensation of a book. I love finishing a book, appreciating where it's taken me. And I also love page one, where you start over, on a new frigate. As Paul Schneider writes in his final sentence of *The Enduring Shore*, "I was glad that the tide, which had brought me in, had washed me out again."

August 2000

REQUIEM

Fifteen years later I can still hear the silence in the synagogue as I stood at the bema and read:

> *Now I was young and easy under the apple boughs/…*
> *happy as the grass was green/…Time let me hail and*
> *climb/Golden in the heydays of his eyes….*

I was reading Dylan Thomas's "Fern Hill" as part of my eulogy for my grandfather because that poem evoked for me the feeling of my grandfather's farm, home to some of my brightest childhood memories.

> *And as I was green and carefree, famous among the*
> *barns/…In the sun that is young once only/Time let*
> *me play and be/Golden in the mercy of his means….*

Images flowed among the pews, and the words filled the sanctuary. We all could picture the farm, stables, pastures, and horses, *spellbound horses walking…On to the fields of praise.*

The rabbi had praised Grandpa and spoken of his gifts as a person. Those words brought back the most memorable gift I had received from him.

Shortly before I turned fourteen, my grandmother had died from cancer, and my birthday was lost in the shuffle of the unhappiness. Two weeks later my grandfather, wearing dark glasses to cover his red eyes, asked me about a gift for my birthday, overlooked but not forgotten, he felt certain I understood.

I don't remember what made me suggest a subscription to *The New York Times*, but I do remember him perking up a bit after I said that. He proceeded to warn me about the *Times*'s liberal bias: It endorsed way too many Democrats; it supported the welfare state; as an antidote, I really should also regularly read *The Wall Street Journal*. But he bought me the subscription.

Then, to ensure a proper balance, he began sending me clips from *The Times* and occasionally *The Wall Street Journal*, something he would do at varying intervals for the next sixteen years. The clips fell into three general categories: Capitalists offer the best hope for a generally unappreciative mankind; inflation should be viewed as the scourge of democracy (and Democrats encourage it); and young people risk becoming miscreants because of society's undue permissiveness.

And I would send him clips, also falling roughly into three categories: Money and Republicans have corrupted the American political system; the military–industrial complex poses almost unfathomable dangers; and flamboyant affectations—long hair, be-ins, Woodstock—reflect positive creative energy, not moral decay.

Mind you, we would never actually express these opinions. Rather, we'd jot a sentence such as, "Thought you'd be interested in the enclosed, in case you missed it." We never convinced the other of anything.

My grandfather never understood his grandchildren's hatred of the needless dying in Vietnam, even though he once sadly shared with me his memory of his younger brother Howard being killed when a milk wagon backed over him on a Brooklyn street near the turn of the century. We almost never mentioned feelings, certainly not our feelings about each other; and though a generational chasm separated us from each other, much of the time, none of this much mattered.

In 1968, when I was eighteen and he was seventy-two, feeling afraid that he might not have many years left (though, as it turned out, he lived to be almost eighty-five) I sent him the best gift I ever gave him—a photograph of myself sitting on the steps of Antioch College's nature preserve, Glen Helen.

That gift, that photograph, made me self-conscious. I had written on it, "To my wonderful grandfather." I think he knew that phrase had taken me, very much my reticent grandfather's grandson, a long time to write. He put my present in the front row of family photographs on the piano in his living room, where it remained for the rest of his life.

My grandfather would live a full life, a long life, but many of his friends had died before him, and at his funeral we all paused at the poet

Dylan Thomas's references to time. *...time would take me...by the shadow of my hand...Time held me green and dying....*

My grandfather lived long enough for his grandchildren to know him—his ironic humor and insufferable rectitude, his caring and his pettiness, his empathic qualities and his incessant, nineteenth-century stiff-upperlipness. I appreciate his most memorable gift to me, his inter-generational and never-spoken-of love. I appreciate it all the more as I see my children receive it in abundance from their grandparents, who all still are living vibrant and healthy lives. Grandpa, as I remember him, is admonishing me to speak of these ties, to talk of love, to value this extraordinary gift for as much time as we may have together and not wait until we again must gather together in such a quiet temple.

February 1995

NOT ABOUT
BASEBALL

MICKEY

The New York Times Pulitzer Prize–winning columnist Anna Quindlen once wrote a piece upbraiding her male colleagues for rhapsodizing over baseball as a somehow-mystical metaphor for life. Think of baseball as a business, she asserted, and ballparks, manicured as they may be, as the means of production, not some metaphysical sanctum.

Credit Quindlen's argument as being spot on. Any rational person would accept her admonition, much as a batter must accept the results of an umpire's call. This piece is not about baseball although it is about Mickey Mantle. Please, before you speed-dial Anna Quindlen, hear me out.

I am a grown-up, I think—who happens to be the proud owner of two Mickey Mantle Topps baseball cards. One hangs on a wall in my law office; the other, encased in plastic, adorns a bookcase in my study at home. My dictionary fittingly defines "Mantle, Mickey Charles" as "American baseball player. One of the greatest sluggers of the game…."

Mantle mattered, and still matters, because he epitomized America's post-war romance with optimism. Nothing felt more magnificent than a Mantle home run—towering, still rising, as it careened into the third deck of Yankee Stadium. And when he struck out, Mantle still made fans feel his intensity, strength, and grace.

Mickey played in pain. We admired that. His knees were ripped apart early in his career when his cleats caught in a drainpipe in the outfield of Yankee Stadium. Surgeons carved up those knees four times. With shredded ligaments and no knee cartilage, he loped to center field because, without miles of bandages wrapped ankle to thigh as tight as on a mummy, he could not take the field at all.

I read this fact in 1958 in the first hardcover book I ever bought. Having saved my allowance for months, I paid for it mostly with quarters.

Two sets of statistics are indelibly etched in my mind: the ones Mantle had, and the ones he would have had, if his spikes hadn't caught in that drainpipe. Lifetime, Mickey batted .298 and hit 537 home runs. A healthy Mantle would have batted .350 and hit 700 homers. I am as sure of the facts that would have been as I am of those that are.

During the Yankees' dynasty, the world remained comfortably predictable. The Bronx Bombers started the season at the top of the American League, picked up a player or two from the Kansas City A's in August, and won easily. Oh, to be sure, the second-place team (depending on the year, the Tigers, Orioles, or Indians—the Red Sox never contended), then behind by four games, would march into Yankee Stadium for a series in early September, but invariably would slink out of town after the Sunday doubleheader trailing by eight.

As long as Mantle roamed center field, we felt comfortable and secure. We had heroes like Mickey Mantle. Life was good.

For some. In the 1950s and early '60s America buried its unquiet memories of the executions of Julius and Ethel Rosenberg. White America ignored or condoned the segregation that *Brown v. The Board of Education* had done precious little to eradicate. And the country glued women in their place as homemakers. Still, at that time, or at least as some remember that time, the beneficence of America felt true.

In 1961, Mantle batted .317 and hit 54 home runs, and President John Kennedy promised us that by decade's end an American would journey to the moon, walk on its surface, and return safely home. In the United States then, anything was possible.

The Yankees' dynasty ended in 1964, the same year Lyndon Johnson campaigned for president promising that he would not send American boys to die in an Asian war.

After 1964, when he should have retired, Mantle lingered in the game for another four years, during which time America burrowed further into the hellhole of Vietnam, and our cities burned. Mickey finally retired in 1968 because, he said, he could no longer run from first to third base on a single. That year, the Kerner Commission, officially the President's National Commission on Civil Disorders, warned that the United

States was splintering into two societies, "one black and one white—separate and unequal."

After he retired, Mickey slid into active alcoholism and lived off his past glory. The editorial encomiums after his death would praise him for eventually facing up to his addiction and encouraging other alcoholics to do the same.

October for some people conjures romantic images—the smell of burning leaves, a foreground of crimson against a backdrop of a rich grey or blue sky, pumpkins by the hundreds by the roadside. But for many of us, October's most romantic image is also a mundane one: not getting caught in study hall, hiding the transistor radio's earpiece in a cupped hand so that Mel Allen's or Red Barber's voice would not escape and betray us. Invariably, though, when Mantle got a hit, a half dozen kids, despite themselves, would blurt out a cheer, and a pile of small radios would end up on the desk of the study hall monitor.

We who were kids then believe in this season because it conjures the feeling of those long-ago, Mantle-filled Octobers. It saddened us, of course, during his last playing years to watch his greatness deteriorate. Still, even then, Mantle's swing remained magnificent, powerful, full of grace, always holding extraordinary promise.

October 1995

WHERE YOU
PLAY THE GAME

There came a time—it kind of crept up on me—when some of my friends' children were no longer just my friends' children, but rather friends in their own right.

Mike Ryan (technically, The Honorable W. Michael Ryan) and his son Luke are two of those people. Mike was a judge who never rolled over for prosecutors and the police. Unlike many judges, he would not accept the testimony of cops when they lied on the stand, and Luke has become one of the best criminal defense and civil rights lawyers in the state—tenacious, dedicated, and effective. Clients love Luke, and judges respect him. Both Ryans are prolific writers—of plays, poetry, and articles. They also are students of history.

I first met Mike when he was a probation officer and Luke when I substituted for him in a writing class that he was teaching at the local jail. To be sure, it is Judy Ryan, Mike's wife and Luke's mother, an elementary school teacher, who is the glue that holds the family together. She also is a friend.

Here is my column about the book that Mike and Luke wrote together.

* * *

The problem with those self-help, understand-yourself books for guys is that the target audience, straight guys, don't read them. And on the off chance they did, they wouldn't actually understand them. If they could and would read and understand those books, they wouldn't need them. Talk about a vicious circle.

Fortunately help has arrived.

It's Where You Played the Game, a book by two Northampton authors named Ryan—W. Michael (day job: judge) and his son Luke (a recent Amherst College grad)—reveals why guys are the way they are: the position a boy played in youth baseball perhaps determines, and certainly prognosticates, everything about his life.

You initially balk at this hypothesis? Well, after reading their book, you won't. The authors base the Ryan Theory of Adolescent Development in American Males on what they assert is "extensive research." Try out these conclusions:

The pitcher. The pitcher is always the best athlete on the team. He is treated like a prima donna and generally will act like one. Forever. He'll marry the homecoming queen, and when their marriage falls apart, she'll be blamed and he'll be forgiven. Gary Hart was a pitcher.

First baseman. First basemen, though excellent athletes, at their core are wannabe pitchers. First basemen pitch only in relief. Despite the enormous success the future inevitably brings them, they always feel a bit sour because they still resent pitchers. They're destined to be number two, and they take the mound only when the real pitcher needs to leave the game. Yale's most famous first baseman was the first George Bush.

The shortstop. The shortstop is a scrappy kid with a bad attitude. The 130-pound high school football middle linebacker, who in the fall exudes great joy when running over 200-pound linemen with his cleats, in warmer weather is a shortstop. Eighty-six percent of Congressional Medal of Honor winners played shortstop. So did Bobby Kennedy. People love shortstops as long as they're not doing hard time.

Second baseman: On the other hand, mothers love second basemen. Genuine and kind, in the field they are always chattering, "Pitcherinthere, youcandoit, youcandoit, pitcherinthere, herewego." They play catch until after dark and later become missionaries or doctors, complete goody-two-shoes. Jimmy Carter played second base all the time. Bill Clinton never did.

The catcher: Unlike other eight-year-old guys, catchers are told they need to wear a cup. This may not mean much to females, but for guys— trust me—this is important. Really important. At age forty, these alleged adults still proudly introduce themselves with nicknames such as "Pudge" and "Hog." They tend to crush your fingers when shaking hands. They're tenacious. Sometimes this is good, sometimes not. J. Edgar Hoover was a catcher.

In his book *Men At Work: The Craft of Baseball*, George Will, the conservative columnist, describes the game as "an activity to be loved...a thing of beauty and a joy forever." OK, not exactly forever, Will later admits, "but at least until the next game, which is much the same thing as forever because seasons stretch into each other." Will then backtracks a bit, lamenting, "I know, I know. Even the continents drift. Nothing lasts. But baseball does renew itself constantly as youth comes knocking at its door, and in renewal it becomes better."

Talk about common ground. The liberal-minded Ryans apparently agree. They write, "While it is often detrimental to the development of self-esteem in American adolescent males to play organized youth baseball, there is something even more perilous—not playing."

Here's the best part of *It's Where You Played the Game*—it's a book the Target Audience guys might actually read. That's good.

But once the guy understands why he is the way he is, what's to be done? Can a pitcher become a second baseman, a first baseman a right fielder? (Right fielders are those boys who never played very well and while in the field tended to count dandelions instead of balls and strikes.)

Although the Ryans leave these vital questions unresolved, they nonetheless allow us to play on a fertile field of hope. Sure, some former shortstops, third basemen, and catchers are daily chest-bumping and crashing into rare historic paintings and chandeliers in the halls of Congress and corporate executive suites, but plenty of former right fielders are ensconced there—and a few of those beloved second basemen as well.

In truth, as guys get older and arms get sorer, many sooner or later play second base, and as the second-base-playing, Red Sox–rooting Ryans write, "This is the year the Red Sox will finally win the World Series." They hurriedly add, "We might not have been right yet, but...for second basemen being loyal is more important than being right."

April 1996

GOLDENS

Calm yourself. Don't put pressure on the kid. It's a long way from here to playing center field for the New York Yankees. I repeated this mantra as I drove our daughter Jo, age six, to her first T-ball practice.

And her last. The first thing the coaches had the kids do was pair up and have a catch. Jo's friend Becky threw the ball to Jo, who put her glove up in the general direction of the ball—which clunked off her forehead—and she walked off the field. No amount of cajoling, importuning, or outward bribery from me could alter what the baseball Gods had wrought.

Our younger daughter Leah's career went further. When she was about eight, I planted a hemlock in our front yard at a place where once we had played Whiffle ball. "You planted a tree on home plate?" Leah demanded to know. "How would you like it if *your father* planted a tree on *your* home plate? What kind of father would plant a tree on home plate?" My realistic points such as, "You can't fit an infield in our yard" and "we still have plenty of room for a catch" made no impression.

My wife Dale, a tomboy in her youth, has always been more than willing to have a catch with me—her baseball glove is well-worn. But some moments that have struck me as a great opportunity for baseball have impressed her as times when the kids should be fed or the hot water heater turned back on.

The net result of all this? For some years when the kids were young, the most reliable member of the household for playing catch with me was our golden retriever, Caboose. Caboose's brain, we were convinced, approximated the size of a tennis ball—because when he saw one, his mind clearly had no room left over for anything else.

Please don't get me wrong, I love goldens—although having lived with one much of my life, I have long harbored doubts about their acumen and indeed often have commiserated with our goldens about their intellectual challenges. (As the writer Christopher Morely said, "No one appreciates the very special genius of your conversation as a dog does.") But now a new book by Stanley Coren, *The Intelligence of Dogs*, says emphatically that my misgivings are misplaced. Professor Coren ranks goldens as the fourth-brightest breed, after border collies, poodles, and German shepherds.

Leaving aside the question of IQ, I think we'd all agree that goldens behave gently and exude a saintly patience with kids. Those traits, combined with their silky coats and deep brown eyes, make them the sentient embodiment of warm and fuzzy. In our house, where everyone has a job, the dog, too, has been assigned responsibilities. The goldens' job—which they have always performed magnificently—is Great Greetings.

Seven years ago Caboose died of cancer. He was only ten. We had known he was dying. In the middle of a night in late October, 'Boose startled Dale and me out of a deep sleep when we heard him struggling his way up the steep back stairs that lead to our bedroom. Bloated from the cancer, he hadn't been able to make it up the stairs for a month or more. Still, at two a.m. he was trying mightily.

We hurried out of bed and took him back down the half dozen stairs he had managed to climb. In the kitchen he laid down, licked me, put his head in Dale's lap, and, having said good-bye, died.

In the backyard before the sun rose and kids woke up, I tried to dig his grave where the irises and violets grow. But that spot had too many roots from the apple tree that once stood there. Next I tried digging in the grass under the kitchen window. There I found ground not rutted with roots and soft enough to dig 'Boose's grave. Cocooned in an old, soft yellow blanket that Dale and I had wrapped around him, he looked like an egg roll. With help from my friends Greg, staying at our house during some construction on his, and Jack, my next-door neighbor, I tucked him into the grave, filled the hole back up, and was surprised to find no dirt left over.

That afternoon the kids in the neighborhood came over and put drawings and cut flowers on the grave and planted spring bulbs in the ground above Caboose's egg-rolled self. We later planted day lilies there as well.

About two years after Caboose died, we found his golden successor in a litter of a friend of a friend. Casey (we named her Casey after, at least in my opinion, the Yankees and Mets manager Casey Stengel) unfortunately seemed compelled to challenge Dr. Coren's findings about goldens by trying, when only a puppy, to bite the front tire of a moving car and doing herself considerable damage. On the other side of the ledger, after Casey passed obedience school—albeit barely—we Scotch-taped her certificate to the baseboard near her cedar chip-stuffed bag bed to remind her of her accomplishment—and her potential. And when it came to playing catch and having a stash of tennis balls around the neighborhood, she needed no schooling or practice—she was a natural.

On a Sunday afternoon this summer, Jo was pushing Leah on a swing, Dale was working in her garden, and I was listening to a baseball game and reading *The New York Times*. Casey, who had been lying near me above the place where 'Boose is buried, stood up, carried her well-salivated tennis ball to me, and dropped it in my lap. When I threw it over her head, she spun around to chase it, but before she could grab it, Dale scooped it up on a hop and threw the ball back to me. The three of us, Dale, Casey, and I had a catch. The girls came over to join us. I was in our backyard in Northampton, Massachusetts, utterly content.

April 1995

WRITE ON!

HAPPY MERRY HANNU-KWANZACHRISTMAS

Every December, wise men and women make a pilgrimage—to an office of the American Civil Liberties Union, including mine in western Massachusetts. They come by letter or in person, by phone or by fax. They arrive bearing questions about God and, more specifically, about some religious display on public property.

Sometimes the caller wants to put one up. Sometimes he or she wants one taken down. Sometimes a municipal official wants to know, more than anything else, how not to get sued.

"What in God's name," they ask—usually in an exasperated tone of voice—"is OK to put up in our [pick one] park, library, city hall? Would you object to a creche? A Christmas tree? How about a menorah? Garlands and wreaths? Any problem with a few reindeer? What about Frosty?"

Sometimes the proposal crosses the constitutional line. Other times it receives the ACLU's blessing. Here's why.

The First Amendment protects freedom of religion in two ways. The Amendment's "free exercise" clause guarantees everyone the right to freely practice (i.e., exercise) his religion. The "establishment clause" of the First Amendment prohibits the government from promoting or assisting or establishing any religion. Religious symbols on public property may trample on the establishment clause.

In the 1980s some residents of Pawtucket, Rhode Island, certainly thought their town had done exactly that—trampled on the establishment clause—by constructing a nativity scene on public property. The federal district court and the United States Court of Appeals both agreed that the town's display had violated the religious freedom protection of the First Amendment. But Pawtucket did not seek forgiveness. Rather, it sought salvation for their legal woes from a higher authority—the United States Supreme Court, which found room on its docket for the case.

The constitutional star that was supposed to guide the justices is the principle that no government—federal, state, or local—may favor any religion. The established law at that time made clear beyond all doubt that a religious display paid for by a city or town and placed on public property crossed the constitutional line. For Pawtucket to win, the court would have to find that Mary, Joseph, and Baby Jesus in the manger did not convey a religious theme.

That's ridiculous—right?

Not according to the Supreme Court. In the 1984 Pawtucket case, the justices appeared to crucify reason on the altar of result, holding that a Santa Claus house, a Christmas tree, and a banner that read "Seanson's Greetings" around the manger transformed that sacred symbol into a secular decoration. Pawtucket's prayers had been answered. The city could keep its creche.

Five years passed. Then, in 1989, two more religious symbol cases were guided to the Supreme Court.

In the first, citizens challenged the government of Allegheny County, Pennsylvania, for placing a manger and magi in the foyer of the courthouse. In the second, taxpayers sued the City of Pittsburgh for erecting in a public park an exhibit consisting of a forty-five-foot-tall Christmas tree, an eighteen-foot-high Hanukkah menorah, and a plaque inscribed with a salute to liberty. (The display lacked a partridge in a pear tree, but, as you'll see, legally that would have helped.)

The 1989 court tepidly resurrected the establishment clause. It held that the Allegheny County crèche, unlike the one in Pawtucket, indeed did violate the establishment clause. The reason? The religious message of the manger had not been diluted sufficiently by secular symbols.

The story of the Christmas tree and the Jewish candelabrum in the park in Pittsburg ended differently. A Christmas tree, the Supreme Court informed us, is not a Christian symbol—news to most Christians, I would think. Similarly, the Hanukkah menorah commemorates an historical, rather than a religious event, undoubtedly news to most Jews, who believe that it symbolizes a miracle from God. Given this, although the manger and the magi had to be removed from the courthouse, Pittsburgh's configuration of symbols in the park could stand. So sayeth the court.

We all understand that the judicial road in the United States ends at the Supreme Court and that the pronouncements of five justices constitute the law. That reality doesn't make the rulings logical or right. It only makes them the law.

For many of us, no matter what the Supreme Court says, a Christmas tree reflects Christmas; a creche cannot be diminished as an important Christian symbol no matter how many secular symbols you stick in the ground around it; a menorah represents a miracle for Jews; and the government has no business in facilitating, paying for, endorsing, or being involved in any of this.

In the annual December brouhahas about religious symbols, we too often lose track of one crucial fact. Churches and private citizens can put up crucifixes and other religious symbols on their private property to their hearts' and souls' delight. The First Amendment protects—absolutely protects—that right.

December brings out proselytizers trying to stretch the boundaries of how much religion the government may promote, people who fervently believe that the government should champion their religion. Conversely, religious displays on public property aggravate, and sometimes enrage, citizens who believe fervently in the Jeffersonian ideal of a wall separating church and state. That's why every holiday season the phone jingles a lot at offices of the American Civil Liberties Union.

The ACLU fields the calls, shepherds them through the legal analysis, and tries to prophesize how a judge may view a particular constellation of figures and symbols placed in a park or a town common or on the portico of a city hall—and decide whether a letter to the powers that be should be written or a lawsuit brought.

In her recent companion book to the PBS documentary *Defending Everybody: A History of the American Civil Liberties Union*, western Massachusetts author and filmmaker Diane Garey relates the story of an ACLU staff member in Virginia who calls the December phenomenon "Manger Mania." That ACLU employee notes that her job requires her to analyze the constitutionality of displays that include a menorah, a creche, Frosty the Snowman, and Rudolph the Red-Nosed Reindeer. Trying to apply the Supreme Court's holiday precedents, the yardstick she uses—one I have found useful in my work for the ACLU—is this: "If Rudolph and Frosty are bigger than the Christ child," she told Garey, "I generally let it go."

December 1998

CONEY ISLAND
IN MY MIND

I am waiting for my case to come up...

and I am waiting for someone
to really discover America
and...
for the war to be fought
which will make the world safe
for anarchy...

and I am perpetually awaiting
a rebirth of wonder....

— *Lawrence Ferlinghetti*

If you're lucky, and I was, you had one teacher in high school who made the whole, tedious, four-year exercise worthwhile. My eleventh- and twelfth-grade English teacher, Blair Torrey, was that person for me. Among the many authors and poets he introduced me to was the beat poet Lawrence Ferlinghetti, not because Mr. Torrey loved him—I'm pretty sure he didn't—but rather because he thought I would.

This spring, Ferlinghetti gave a reading to 1400 people at Smith College. At eighty-two, his voice is still strong. He is tall and wears deep red, oversized reading glasses. He has written fourteen collections of poetry, as well as novels, plays, and translations. His also paints prolifically, continues as the publisher of City Light Books, and, as I found out the next day, carries his own bag when he travels. Local poet and writer Anna Kirwan arranged for us to spend a few hours driving him to Boston.

In the car and later at the Cafe Paradiso in Boston's North End, where we had espresso and cappuccino before he caught his plane to San Francisco, we talked about Ezra Pound and anti-Semitism, Allen Ginsberg, Richard Brautigan, Robert Bly, and the Sandinista poets Daisy Zamora, Rosario Murillo, and Roberto Vargas; the Mount Hermon School (which Ferlinghetti's parents shipped him off to after he, as he said, "filched a dime"); poetry slams and censorship; his trip to an international poetry festival in Delphi, Greece; his time as poet laureate of San Francisco; the economics of writing; the ACLU; travel; and soccer. And column writing.

On the Mass Pike, somewhere around Sturbridge, Ferlinghetti mentioned that he writes a column for the *San Francisco Chronicle*. He and I then commiserated about the plight of column writers, the strictures of word length, and the tyranny of newspaper staffers who can lop off a perfectly constructed paragraph to save an inch, and feel no remorse.

I mentioned to Ferlinghetti that I'd written a piece for the *Daily Hampshire Gazette* (which appears later in this section) about why and how to write a column. He invited me to send him a copy, which I did.

Ferlinghetti's handwritten note back said, "Your column on columns took the words right out of my mouth!" He then wrote, "I'd only add, 'Try to shock them.'" And then, turning to the practical, he added, "And if you write something shocking, try to get it past the editor."

July 2001

TYPOOS

[Here's] what lies ahead. "Plywood" will become "playwool," "fisherman" will become "figbun," "Hibernia" become[s] "hernia."

The *Daily Hampshire Gazette* often reminds me of this description of the *Gammy Bird*, the small-town newspaper in E. Annie Proulx's novel *The Shipping News*.

My recent column about Jews and Ireland attempted to reference the *pogroms* that Jews have suffered throughout history. However, as printed on the *Gazette's* editorial page, I came out foursquare against Jewish *programs*.

"Now," Buggit [the editor] said, "you're working at this newspaper, which does pretty good… but typos are part of the Gammy Bird."

When typeset in the *Gazette*, my column about Mike and Luke Ryan's book, *It's Where You Played the Game*, by leaving out some words, turned one reasonably fine-tuned sentence into a discordant and unconnected subordinate clause. I consider this a minor literary indignity compared with the reprint in the *Massachusetts Lawyers Weekly*, which had me chatting about the foibles of catchers, shortstops and third base*ments.*

This is a column, bellowed [Gammy Bird writer] Quoyle. You can't change somebody's column….

We expect a lot from a local newspaper. We feel entitled to have it guide us through the fug of local boards, commissions, and town meetings, and to six times a week tell us what's going on around here and, hopefully, to not turn the word fug into fog or fudge or fugue.

Local papers matter. Former *Daily Hampshire Gazette* editor Ed Shanahan's recent article in the *Boston Globe Magazine* about the death of the *Holyoke Transcript-Telegram* quoted a lifelong resident of that nearby city who likened that paper's demise to someone hitting the mute button in the middle of a television program. Another resident compared the city without its paper to "a tent without its centerpost."

Like the *Gammy Bird*, here in Northampton and the surrounding towns, the *Gazette* occupies a central place. It has published continuously since 1786.

Near the end of *The Shipping News*, after the editor has died, the central character, Quoyle, is asked, "Will the *Gammy Bird* be put to rest?" And Quoyle answers, "No. A paper has a life of its own."

Hopefully Quoyle has it right.

* * *

I have to tell you—though Quoyle might be right, Ferlinghetti was way too optimistic. The *Daily Hampshire Gazette* refused to run the column you just read, which, in its original form, supplied some more examples of typos in the paper. The editor bellowed at me that he wasn't paying me "good money" (thirty dollars per column) to criticize his newspaper.

"But the point of the column is how important your local paper is to the community, not the number of typos," I argued. "And really, it's unbelievably gentle, don't you think?" The answer was, No, he didn't think.

The following month my in-the-doghouse standing with the paper deteriorated further when the column I submitted—about the porn star Annie Sprinkle—began by telling this story: *When I arrived home after work one day last week, my wife asked me if anything interesting had happened that day and I replied, "Not much, except for spending the afternoon staring at Annie Sprinkle's cervix."*

Ok, there was a little literary license there. I actually hadn't spent that afternoon staring at the entrance to Annie's uterus—that would have to wait until the actual show—but basically, what I wrote was accurate. Annie would invite the audience to come up to the stage to do exactly that—to look at her uterus with a speculum, what she called her "Public Cervix Announcement," part of her "Post-Post-Porn-Modernist" show. I know this as the lawyer for WOW, the production company sponsoring Annie.

There was nothing untoward or titillating in what I had written, but the editorial page editor, with even greater emphasis than the managing editor the month before, informed me that my choice was either to have the column published without the offending first sentence or to not have it published at all.

Still, why not take a joust or two at a windmill? "The problem is what?" I demanded to know. "The word speculum is a perfectly fine word, I've written an accurate description of the performance, and I'm not responsible for readers' febrile imaginations." My arguments, not unexpectedly, accomplished exactly nothing.

Better to be able to describe some porn than none, I thought, and my duly censored article was published with a new, more antiseptic beginning (albeit with the words "speculum" and "vagina" in the first paragraph).

In the end I felt bad, as if I had disappointed Mr. Ferlinghetti. I consoled myself with the adage that if you really want freedom of the press, you need to own a press.

December 1996

Postscript

It helps to like the editor and vice versa. Notwithstanding these tiffs, the *Gazette* continued to publish my column for another six years, when I exited on my own.

ANNIE RETURNS

Porn star Annie Sprinkle is back in the news because the Northampton Center for the Arts is reneging on its commitment to showcase her newest performance piece, "Hard Core from the Heart." Why would the Center do that?

Let me count the ways.

The center's director first claimed that undercover Northampton police attending Annie's performance at the Northampton Lesbian Festival in 1995 had concluded that Sprinkle had violated the state obscenity laws, but—and only as a matter of discretion and good taste—had decided not to press charges. In response, the police chief has categorically denied that any officer, undercover or covered, had been assigned to attend the performance. (Maybe everyone's telling the truth. Perhaps the cops went to the show but not while on duty?—just a thought.)

The center's director then expressed her fear that the police would be staring at Annie eagle-eyed for any possible transgression. Not so, says the police chief. His cops would be patrolling the streets looking for crime, not sitting on their duffs in a theater examining Annie's body parts.

After that, the center pleaded an inability to ensure that everyone in the audience would be over eighteen. This excuse was stripped of its efficacy when it was pointed out that audiences' IDs had been checked at Annie's six previous sold-out performances in Northampton without any problems.

The Center for the Arts next offered potential legal liability as a justification for banning Annie. In response, Sprinkle stated, "It's absurd to worry about legal action. I don't even take my clothes off in the show. There are sexual scenes on film"—she does a monologue in front of the film—"but they're no different than the ones you buy or rent in any video store." The performance, she explained, promotes healing and "uses art to explore fear, confusion, and pain surrounding sex."

It would have been better for the center's director to not try to cover up her prudishness and instead admit the naked truth—that she just didn't want Annie on her stage—instead of banning her for transparently flimsy reasons. The center's censoring of Annie has, however, benefitted us—by stimulating a discussion in our community about erotica, pornography, and obscenity. Here's a quick synopsis so that you can sound erudite when explaining why you went to her show.

Pornography means sexually explicit material. Porn is sometimes used erroneously as a synonym for "obscenity," but that's wrong. Obscenity is the totally gross stuff. Most porn is not obscene.

Erotica: If a sexually explicit movie, video, or book turns you on, it's erotica. If it offends you, it's pornography. If you didn't understand it, maybe it's just art. One person's erotic art may strike someone else as smutty trash. In general, think of erotica as toney porn.

Obscenity: At the far end of the continuum of sexually explicit material, an unclear line divides nudity, erotica, and pornography from obscenity. Legally the not-always-clear boundary that separates porn from obscenity matters a lot. The First Amendment guarantees our right to create, read, and view all sorts of erotic books and pornographic movies, but it doesn't protect obscenity. Obscenity, legally, is the portrayal of sexually explicit conduct that, taken as a whole, appeals to your prurient interest and utterly lacks any serious literary, artistic, political, or scientific value. Prurient, more or less, means lascivious, which, more or less, means salacious. Got that? Clear enough?

Of course not. The difficult, if not impossible, task of rationally applying that definition to the breasts and buttocks in the record before him caused Supreme Court Justice Potter Stewart to blurt out in a concurring opinion one of the most famous lines ever written by a Supreme Court Justice: "But I know it when I see it." Because Justice Stewart is no longer with us to tell us what he sees, for convenience sake, think of obscenity as the sexually explicit stuff that totally, completely, and utterly grosses you out and, you're pretty sure, absolutely everyone else, including the most liberal dude you know.

Annie's new show articulates one feminist critique and constitutes social commentary. That's why even though the excerpts from her X-rated movies show some explicit and coarse sexual activity, the local police have correctly concluded that the First Amendment protects her from the law's prying eyes.

Further good news: we need not get mawkish about our local Center for the Arts's affront to artistic freedom. The Pearl Street Night Club has announced that it will happily present Annie, so the show will go on.

Annie will be with us. We'll see if some clothes come off. It's all good.

February 1997

DON'T TRUST COLUMNISTS!

Columnists are trying to manipulate us and our opinions. Here's how they do it.

They begin by trying to make you think that they are on the same team with us. Here, I've referred to columnists as "they" and we readers as "us" so that we all know whose side I'm on.

Still with me? Let's go on. Please. (Columnists, however dogmatic, want you to think they sound reasonable and polite).

A column is, in essence, an essay. In their book, *Thinking on Paper*, Harvard University professors Vernon Howard and James Barton instruct that we should think of an essay's opening paragraph as a triangle pointed down. The opening thought—the long top-side of the triangle—states the essay's major point: columnists are manipulative. The next sentence directs the reader into the analysis: "Here's how they do it."

Credibility, of course, is critical. A columnist wants the reader to believe that his point, his thesis, is supported by weighty authority. Invoking Harvard always helps.

To gain trust, experts advise the writer to grapple with arguments contrary to his position. While I can't completely concur with this approach, the technique does—trust me on this—demonstrate the writer's fair-mindedness.

The experts also recommend using three examples to prove a point. One or two lack heft. Four sound like a campaign speech. Three sound right. Just listen: Three Bears, Three Little Pigs, three strikes and you're out.

Likewise, a one-sentence paragraph can really pack a punch. Try this one.

Short sentences work.

Mr. Murphy, my junior high school teacher who forbade one-sentence paragraphs, also taught us to never split infinitives and to always avoid alliteration. And I still remember Mr. Murphy trying to pound into our Silly-Puttied brains the proposition that conjunctions such as "and" and "but" should never begin a sentence, and never, ever begin a paragraph.

But a paragraph that begins with a conjunction can grab your attention. Mr. Murphy, I now surmise, never had to write a column.

Some rules that Mr. Murphy taught do indeed improve writing. For example, passive verb constructions should not be used. Intransitive verbs are boring. A sentence that ends with a preposition is something to be ashamed of. "Eschew cliches," he would say. "They're a dime a dozen." He also lectured repeatedly on the evils of redundancy.

As you can see, transitions matter. Sometimes the writer can entice you to read on by promising sex later in the column. Generally, I, of course, wouldn't stoop to that level, but here I will.

Fine, you say. But what about substance?

Well, that's a tough question, so let's skip it for a moment and observe that a question may make a transition seem seamless. Did you notice?

In addition, the at-ease interjection "well" makes us feel as if the writer and reader are old friends chatting over espresso in a sidewalk cafe. As the New York Yankees announcer Mel Allen used to say, "Well, how about that!"

Finally, note that an analogy, like strong coffee, opens our eyes and makes us see a picture more clearly. We like analogies.

For the answer to the tough question, I'll rely on Anna Quindlen, the Pulitzer Prize–winning former *New York Times* columnist. In her collection *Thinking Out Loud*, Quindlen explains that for her, "The truth is, the reader I write for is myself…." As for motivation and ideas, "When I am deeply aggrieved," she says, "I can never type fast enough." Her advice for column writing: know something, care deeply, and pray you're not too wrong too often.

Of course, the reader can't agree with the writer's conclusion if he has put the paper down, or flipped to another, more promising story, before he gets to it. This means that the writer's primary, albeit pedestrian, goal is to keep the reader reading. Please note that the part about sex is coming up really soon although, to appreciate it, you need to know this: An essay's ending, according to professors Howard and Barton (who, by the way, borrowed the idea from a 1965 book by Lucile Vaughan Payne titled *The Lively Art of Writing*), should reverse the analytical triangle with which the piece began. The top of the triangle, which connects to the internal argument, should broaden out at the end to rest upon a more universal conclusion.

George Will, the politically conservative columnist, titled his collection of columns about baseball *Bunts* because columns are like bunts, which Will defines as "modest and often useful things, [that] are not always well understood, even by those who are supposed to know when and how to lay them down." I agree, but after five years of writing them, here's what I think I understand.

First, writing a column is a learning experience. It forces me to figure out what I really think about a politician, a policy, or an event. At some point, usually as a deadline is approaching, I have to commit to the words and thoughts. Drafts are like dates—you wish you could go out on a few more before you move in together.

Second, a column requires immersion in a creative process—something that brings me back to the movement of the 1960s. Creativity was part of its soul, and as Emma Goldman said, "If I can't dance, I don't want to be part of your revolution."

Finally, a column allows me to try to convince you—and others—with my words. There's plenty of joy and a good dollop of ego in that.

But column-writing is not one long *kumbaya* moment. Deadlines loom. Page designers zealously enforce word counts. Editors use garden shears on delicately crafted paragraphs.

And one omnipresent problem exacerbates all the others—a point the progressive, syndicated columnist Ellen Goodman made during a formal speech at Stanford University (Stanford works almost as well as Harvard). In that talk Goodman analogized column-writing to nymphomania, explaining that you've barely finished one piece before you're on to the next.

November 1999

THE MORE
THINGS CHANGE

PRIDE DAY 2013

In February, the Northampton police chief refused to issue a permit for the Gay Rights Parade in early May, asserting that his department could not "handle traffic problems caused by a march of more than 200 people on a Saturday." The mayor and a majority of the city council stood shoulder to shoulder with the chief in backing that decision.

The year of that pronouncement, appropriately, was 1984. At that time the city's parade ordinance gave the police chief unreviewable power to allow or deny a permit for a parade of 200 or more people. So the chief had the law of the city on his side.

But the parade organizers had the First Amendment on theirs. As march organizer Kim Christianson put it, "People shouldn't be denied their freedom of speech and right to assemble on a certain day of the week." The ACLU agreed and sued the city, and in April 1984, a state superior court judge struck down that unconstitutional ordinance and ordered the city to issue the parade permit. Two thousand people marched that year, although many wore paper bags over their heads—fearful of being recognized, ostracized from their families, and fired from their jobs.

In 1980, the ACLU, GLAD (Gay and Lesbian Advocates and Defenders), my law partner, Wendy Sibbison, and I argued Bunny King's gay custody case, a guardianship fight, at the Massachusetts Supreme Judicial Court (SJC), and won. In 1983, the SJC applied that equality principle to divorce cases. Six years later, in 1989, Massachusetts passed a law prohibiting discrimination on the basis of sexual orientation in employment, housing, and public accommodations. The next year, 1990, the Massachusetts Department of Social Services changed its policies so that gays and lesbians could become foster parents on the same basis as heterosexual adults. And in 1993 the SJC ruled that gays and lesbians had equal rights to adopt children as well.

The year 2003 brought the biggest victory of all when our state's highest court ruled 4 to 3 that our state constitution guarantees gay couples the same right to marry as heterosexuals, making our Commonwealth the first state to legalize marriage equality. Now there are ten. Soon there will be twelve.

As goes Massachusetts, so goes the nation? If only it were that easy. In 1996, President Clinton signed into law the Defense of Marriage Act (DOMA), which defines marriage for purposes of federal law as between one man and one woman only. Since then, thirty-eight states have enacted similar laws or constitutional provisions.

The United States Supreme Court will hand down decisions in two gay marriage cases before the end of this term. In those cases the court could leave no doubt that all prohibitions on gay marriage violate the constitutional guarantee of equal protection. Don't count on it.

The high court also could write opinions that favor marriage equality but then limit the reach of those decisions by holding that the states, not the federal government, have the right to define marriage. It could well hold in the California case that the decision applies only to California. Such opinions would leave marriage equality to be battled out state by state. The court also could rule, 5 to 4, that the federal constitution guarantees no protection at all for gay and lesbian couples who want to marry.

Regardless of what the supreme court decides, the fight for lesbian, gay, bisexual, and transgender (LGBT) rights will continue. Frank Bruni, in a recent *New York Times* column, addressed his readers who have been grousing about his consistent and adamant advocacy for LGBT rights. Bruni promised that he would cease and desist his advocacy just as soon as a few things happen, specifically: that "a gay, lesbian or transgender kid isn't at special risk of committing suicide;" that "the federal government outlaws discrimination on the basis of sexual orientation;" that "...coaches don't hurl basketballs at players' heads while yelling 'faggot';" and "when our relationships aren't relegated to a lesser status, a diminished dignity." Fittingly, the Northampton Pride Committee chose as the theme for this year's march, with its anticipated more than 20,000 participants, "Our Journey Is Not Complete."

May 2013

BENCHGATE

"I'll be waiting for you by our bench," my wife, Dale, told me on the phone.

When I met her a half hour or so later, sensing something amiss, I immediately asserted, "I'm on time," modified quickly by, "more or less." Then, to forestall any focus on my chronic untimeliness I added the verbal feint, "But I'm here."

"But it's not."

"What's not?"

"The bench."

In my mind I quickly counted the times that day I had walked by that spot and not noticed that our bench had vanished, replaced by memory and vacant space over a concrete slab in the brick part of the sidewalk. Of course, it's not really our bench. It's the city's, and we share it with the community. When I was a kid, my friends and I had a meeting place. Our bench gave Dale and me an adult version of that.

Being ever helpful, I asked, "Who would steal our bench?"

But, it turns out, six benches in downtown Northampton were not stolen under cover of darkness. Rather, they were removed by the city's Business Improvement District—under cover of darkness. The BID claimed that too many people (by which they meant too many poor, disheveled, and homeless people) were plopping themselves and their stuff down on them for too long, and those people had to go, which meant the benches had to be disappeared.

Per executive order, those six benches, alleged to be the worst of the worst, were removed without notice or a hearing and secretly transported to a secure government facility, where, behind high fences and multiple locks, they have been indefinitely detained.

The primary motivation for removing the benches? The desire of some business owners to rid downtown of people who, they assert, make potential shoppers uncomfortable and dissuade them from patronizing their stores or even visiting the city.

This thesis is not self-evident. After all, many people come to Northampton to observe the parade of humanity. Shoppers who wish to stroll in an antiseptic, homogenized, air-conditioned, humidity-controlled, cookie-cutter-created environment that displays no blemishes of societal discord and plays Muzak instead of music already can frequent one of the close-by malls.

And certain panhandlers are genuinely enjoyed (certainly tolerated without complaint, anyway) by many, if not most, downtown patrons and those business owners—local boys and girls collecting for their sports teams; Planned Parenthood seeking members and money; political canvassers requesting your signatures and cash; and the Salvation Army bell-ringers shaking their bells for contributions at Christmastime, among others.

In 1997, the Massachusetts Supreme Judicial Court, in striking down the state's anti-begging law, ruled that for First Amendment purposes there is no difference between those who solicit for organized charities and those who ask for alms for themselves. The state's highest court said that a listener's annoyance or offense cannot dilute the First Amendment guarantee of the right to ask for help. After all, the court reasoned, people are free to walk away from a beggar's request.

But what about crime? Some business owners assert that panhandlers commit assault and battery or harassment, make threats, block entrances, and impede pedestrians—and that the police aren't there to help. The police counter that if they aren't called, how can they respond? And besides, they're running low on available officers. Here's how to resolve this longstanding, sometimes bitter dispute.

If panhandlers actually pose a crime problem, a cop downtown on foot or bike patrol would more than likely solve it, so why not take the cop out of the Northampton schools and put an additional officer downtown during daylight hours? After all, as the police department's response to a recent public records request shows, the cop whose job it is to hang out at the schools has made a total of two arrests on school grounds in all of 2012 and 2013, both for minor misdemeanors. The police chief calls that fully armed and uniformed cop a "school resource officer." How about we have a community resource officer instead?

After a week in exile ("Free The Bench Six!" our neighborhood listserve proclaimed) the benches now are being returned to their places of origin. But the reasons that motivated their removal still remain.

Discomfort, I suggest, is at the heart of the matter—an understandable discomfort. When you are passing a panhandler, do you avoid his gaze and pretend you don't see him? Do you wonder whether she's scamming you? Or walk faster to make your uneasiness dissipate quicker? All of the above?

On the way to lunch at a restaurant, who wants to be asked ten times for money so that, according to the panhandler anyway, he or she might eat? I work hard eight or ten or twelve hours a day, you may say to yourself? Can't I just enjoy my lunch hour?

At some level of consciousness, encountering a panhandler forces us, the privileged, to acknowledge that there, but for the fortuity of birth family, the beneficence of others, and good fortune, go I. We are in effect being forced to acknowledge, perhaps against our will, perhaps at an inconvenient or stressful time, that we have no God-given right to the comfortable chairs and couches on which we sit most hours in our day when others don't have chairs—or a home—at all. Begging makes the economic schism, the discordant reality, impossible to ignore. It forces us to acknowledge the thin sliver of happenstance that separates those of us who are being asked from those who are doing the asking. As Napoleon Bonaparte said, "A throne is only a bench covered with velvet."

June 2013

TAKE A WARNING

Take a warning: this story is graphic and despicable.

So begins Elizabeth Reid's article in a recent *Yale Law Journal*. Her next sentence: *Rape always is.*

Reid weaves her story of being raped between the enumerated paragraphs of the complaint (a complaint is the paper that begins a civil law suit) in *Doe v. Clark*, a Washington state case. That class action alleged multiple sexual assaults at Department of Corrections facilities for women, failure to protect those women, inaction by officials with the responsibility of investigating sexual assaults, and retaliation against women who dared to take on the system and actually report them.

Interspersed between the dry statements of the legal theories, Ms. Reid describes being raped while serving time. And what happened. And what didn't.

In 2006, when Reid was two and a half months away from wrapping up her three-year prison sentence in Washington state, she was transferred to a halfway house, a huge step toward freedom. She felt ecstatic. But not for long. There a male staff member ordered her to help him carry some pillows and blankets. She did as instructed. *"What was I supposed to do?"* she writes, *"Disobey a direct order?"* He walked her into a storage closet.

> *I can still hear the keys jangling as he turned them*
> *in the lock of the door. Something awful was about*
> *to happen. I knew this as surely as I knew my own*
> *name.... I can still hear the click.*

As he locked the door and took out a prophylactic, she negotiated and pleaded and resisted as best she could.

*When he was finished with me, I ran to the bathroom
and threw up until I dry heaved. When I got in the
shower and started scrubbing, I couldn't stop.*

Reid didn't report the rape.

If she had, in accord with the long-established protocol, she would
have been shipped back to the prison and thrown into the hole—solitary
confinement—for the rest of her sentence. The system, by guaranteeing the immediate punishment of the victim, assured that few rapes and
sexual assaults would be reported. As a prisoner, there was nothing Elizabeth Reid could do.

*We kept quiet. Over and over again. We kept quiet. I
had felt helplessness in my life before prison. But I had
to go to prison to understand what true powerlessness
was.*

Reid's rape was not an isolated incident. To the contrary, a pandemic
of rape runs rampant in our prisons. A recent government study reports
216,000 prison rapes and sexual assaults per year and cautions that that
number, which seeks to include guard-on-inmate and inmate-on-inmate
sexual assaults, probably underreports the actual number.

Reid held on to the hope of finding justice. After all, unlike most inmate rape victims, she was nearing the end of her sentence, and she had
dramatic proof. The case, unlike many, would not be her word against his
because the rapist-guard had distinguishing marks on his legs that could
be seen only with his pants down.

But the civilian cops wouldn't investigate their brother law enforcement officer. As Reid states succinctly, *"Law enforcement won't serve
and protect me. I am a felon."*

A decade ago, the U.S. Congress peeked behind the razor wires and
enacted the nice-sounding Prison Rape Elimination Act. This is how Reid
sees that law:

The prison administration vigorously publicizes the Prison Rape Elimination Act (PREA). They tell us we have rights... [that] they are there to help us. It even sounds noble... as if they believe what they are saying.... [But] under the cloak of the PREA, things have not changed.

Prison and government officials have spent ten years ignoring that law, and Reid's article spotlights how only through the extraordinary efforts of a handful of prisoners'-rights lawyers and advocates has the law been enforced at all. The Washington case shows us one example.

That litigation resulted in the state paying millions of dollars in damages and legal fees and firing some guards. In addition, the state was required to install video surveillance cameras in secluded areas at institutions where the guards have preyed on inmates. Women who report rapes no longer will be shipped to segregation, and actual investigations will be conducted.

This law review article, which at its core constitutes a testament to human resilience, nonetheless leaves us feeling the dread Reid felt and still feels. It begins, *"The turn of a lock... I'm back in that room. Locked in the room that is the subject of sweats and nightmares that shake me from my sleep. Even now, five years later."* And it ends, *"My rapist will never be held accountable. He got away with it. And me? Well, I may be free, but I got a life sentence."*

Elizabeth Reid, who graduated from community college this spring and will be attending the University of Washington in the fall, now works as a prisoners'-rights advocate. Her long-term goal is to become a lawyer specializing in public policy and social justice.

July 2013

GEORGE ZIMMERMAN AND TRAYVON MARTIN

Some people are saying we've heard and debated enough about George Zimmerman and Trayvon Martin. But before agreeing, can we recall the magazine advertisement that ran some years ago that showed photographs of two men's faces side by side—one black, one white—with the question, which man is the criminal?

Knowing this had to be a trick question, you searched futilely for any telltale signs of gang membership or evidence that one may have been beaten up in prison. Perhaps one was wearing a smirk that demonstrated his predilection for antisocial behavior? At the bottom of the ad the answer was revealed.

The answer was neither. Or both.

The photographs, you see, were identical—except that in one, the color of the man's skin was white and in the other, black. The lesson? It is difficult to look beyond race even when we are struggling mightily to do that, and it's particularly difficult when we are talking about crime and punishment.

Here's another, more chilling, example. A 1983 study by University of Iowa College of Law Professor David Baldus, which examined every homicide in Georgia, demonstrated that only two factors determine whether a jury condemned a defendant to death row—the race of the defendant and the race of the victim.

A defendant being black instead of white doubles his chances of being sentenced to death. But the race of victim matters even more.

Baldus's research team found that when the victim was white instead of black the defendant was four times more likely to be executed. The original Baldus study has been replicated in a dozen states, both north and south, with the same results.

Equally troubling, the racism imbued in our system of capital punishment does not stand out as an aberrational part of our system of criminal justice, but rather is emblematic of it. Recent FBI data regarding marijuana offenses, for example, shows that across America, blacks are arrested for pot at a rate 400 percent greater than whites, even though everyone uses marijuana at about the same rate. And, when it comes to dangerous illegal drugs, the story gets even worse.

Consider cocaine. Crack and powder cocaine are equally addictive. The difference between them is that crack is most frequently sold and used in black ghettos, while powder is the cocaine of choice in white suburbs. For years the Federal Sentencing Guidelines required crack cocaine users (blacks) to be imprisoned 100 times longer than powder cocaine offenders (whites) for equivalent amounts of the drug. The Fair Sentencing Act, enacted by Congress in 2010, reduced the disparity from 100-to-1 to 18-to-1.

Defenders of George Zimmerman's acquittal point out that the critics did not sit in court, view all the evidence, and hear all the testimony and arguments and, further, that the prosecutors with their poor performance may well have failed to establish proof beyond a reasonable doubt. That argument sounds logical but fails to acknowledge the import of emotion in a jury verdict. Here the jurors clearly empathized with the defendant, George Zimmerman, and not with the victim, Trayvon Martin. This perspective also ignores the overarching truth that the entire system failed Trayvon Martin.

Try this fact pattern: At night a black teenager in a hoodie and carrying a loaded firearm is following a white man in three-piece suit. The most dangerous thing in the white man's possession is a candy bar, apt to increase his cholesterol. The black teenager believes the white man is a real estate guy, coming into his neighborhood to rip off his family and his neighbors. A police officer twice instructs the teenager to stop his stalking and surveillance but to no avail. The black kid confronts the white man, a fight breaks out, and the black kid shoots the white man dead.

Under these circumstances would you expect the police to undertake a serious investigation? Would the black teenager have been brought into custody and immediately interrogated? Would charges quickly have been brought? Would the jury likely conclude that if somehow the black teenager was not guilty of murder or manslaughter, that he was at least guilty of something?

In the mid-1980s I met Warren McCleskey—a polite, soft-spoken young man who was deeply remorseful for his crime—and his lawyer in the attorney–client visiting room for death row inmates at the state prison in Jackson, Georgia. McCleskey was black, the victim of his crime was white, and his appeal—based on the Baldus study—was heading to the supreme court.

In its decision, the nine Supreme Court justices unanimously accepted the Baldus study as accurate, but five of them expressed the fear that if they overturned McCleskey's conviction on the basis of the racism in the administration of capital punishment, other people of color subjected to dicrimination in other parts of the criminal system would seek justice at the supreme court as well. That result—too many people seeking too much justice—struck five justices as intolerable.

McCleskey lost 5 to 4. On September 26, 1991, he was strapped into the electric chair, electrodes were attached to his skull, a final prayer was read, and he was executed.

The media has been offering nonstop coverage and commentary on the now-acquitted George Zimmerman and the deceased Trayvon Martin, and I understand the feeling some people have expressed, that the media has reported everything there is to report, every possible opinion has been opined, and that enough is enough. That's probably true, and so I pledge to stop harping about the case and the next one like it—just as soon as the criminal justice system stops being broken and racist.

August 2013

WOMEN AND
MAMMON AT SMITH

On Saturday, June 6, 1981, the lead editorial in *The Boston Globe*, titled "Women and Mammon at Smith," excoriated the college for its treatment of its low-paid food service and housekeeping staff. It focused on the fight at that time between those employees and the college over their pension.

And rightfully so.

Smith, for years, had taken the position that the pension was more than adequate, generous even. Under that plan a service staff employee who retired after thirty years would receive a maximum of about 135 dollars per month, and very few retired long-term service workers received more than 1100 dollars a year.

The Globe pointedly summarized, "Smith is exploiting low-paid employees who cook [and] clean." The paper found "inexcusable" the fact that the college, which boasts of Gloria Steinem and Betty Friedan—the mothers of modern feminism—as alumnae, could so poorly compensate its long-term women service employees. Such treatment, the newspaper asserted, eviscerates "any high-minded, academic talk about equality for women" and lends credence to the criticism of the women's movement as elitist, promoting the interests of the well-heeled while ignoring the struggles of their working-class sisters.

Fast forward to today. With regard to its treatment of housekeepers and food service workers, mostly women and generally the lowest paid people on the campus, Smith has now allowed another unfairness to fester.

In real terms, those employees are earning less today than they were a decade ago. But that's just the tip of the iceberg.

In addition to wages, a major issue this year in the now-stalled negotiations between the union—comprised of these Smith employees only—and the college is the cost of health insurance. These employees participate in Smith's health insurance plans on the same basis as all other employees, which may sound pretty good until you understand what it means.

Consider the woman whose job it is to take care of the dining room, who has worked at Smith for eleven years and earns 22,000 dollars in her nine-month job (no work during summer is guaranteed, and such work as there is is mostly part-time). She ends up paying about half her salary for her contribution to a family health insurance plan. The 175,000 dollars-per-year administrator pays the same amount.

Not long ago housekeepers and food service workers at Smith numbered 260. Now there are 132. The Dining Service employees are serving the same number of students with half the previous staff. In addition, they necessarily are working harder because they now prepare many more specialized meals—kosher, halal, vegetarian, vegan, and gluten-free, among others.

The food service operation, part of the house system at Smith, is unique and plays an important part in the college's marketing campaigns to attract students. At Smith, the cooks prepare all the meals, literally from soup to nuts, providing restaurant-quality food three times a day at every house that serves meals. This is not an assembly-line food operation—it's anything but that. And these workers have great pride as professionals, and are extraordinarily loyal to the college and the students.

In past years and until other obligations intervened, I assisted these employees in their contract negotiations. When I recently learned how Smith was stonewalling the workers this year, I was saddened but not surprised. During the last negotiation in which I participated, we could not even agree whether Smith has an obligation to pay these women a living wage.

Smith boasts an endowment of $1.6 billion, an increase since 2005 of $600 million, and has income of nearly $300 million a year. It can afford to pay a living wage.

Smith has much to be proud of—a dedicated faculty, smart students, a beautiful campus, an exceptional group of alums—which makes its treatment of its housekeeping and food service workers all the more painful to witness, all the more difficult to reconcile with the mission of the college.

In her will Sophia Smith stated that the mission of the institution that bears her name would be to provide for women "an education equal to that afforded to young men." She envisioned a college where women's "wrongs would be redressed, their wages adjusted, their weight of influence in reforming the evils of society...greatly increased." As *The Globe* editorial in 1981 concluded, "Her institution has sadly proved her wrong."

The collective bargaining agreement between the college and the housekeeping and food service workers expired at the beginning of this summer. On the issue of wages and health insurance, after six months of negotiations, the college has barely budged.

The negotiations continue. Still to be answered is whether in 2013 Sophia Smith's institution, by emulating the corporate model that the rich get richer as workers become poorer, sadly will prove her wrong again.

October 2013

TOO HOT FOR HAMPSHIRE

The Sidebar

In 1988 I called the distinguished civil liberties lawyer Harvey Silverglate for advice: should I accept the offer to open and run an ACLU office in Northampton? Harvey told me I should, "because," he explained, "as an ACLU lawyer you get to dance with angels."

The phone had hardly settled back in its cradle before two University of Massachusetts groups, Students for America and the Young Republican Club, called. The university had nixed their plan to sponsor a speech on campus by the country's leading gay-basher, the defrocked psychologist Paul Cameron, during Gay Pride Week. They wanted to know, would the ACLU defend their First Amendment right to have Cameron speak at UMass?

The conversation made me sick to my stomach. I couldn't dial Silverglate fast enough. "Harvey, there is something I really need to ask you," I said after telling him about the phone call. "Where the fuck are the angels?"

At that time administrators at the university's flagship campus in Amherst were busy justifying their censorship of Cameron by claiming that the sponsoring student groups needed to pay for, but couldn't afford, the cost of adequate security. UMass had trotted out this canard once before—a decade earlier—when administrators attempted to prohibit Black Panther Angela Davis from speaking.

The university ultimately relented and let Davis speak. And similarly, in 1988, UMass declined the invitation I extended on behalf of the ACLU—to let a federal court decide whether recognized student organizations at a public university, supposedly devoted to the free marketplace of ideas, have the right to present a speaker of their choice—regardless of how unpopular, controversial, or reviled.

When Cameron arrived on campus the next week, he was greeted with the largest—at that time—gay-rights demonstration ever held in western Massachusetts, editorials condemning him and his views, teach-ins, and LGBT support services—all of which helped galvanize the LGBT community.

Consider the paradigm. The way to expose, confront, and root out bad, bigoted, and hateful speech is not through censorship, but rather with more, better, and righteous speech. In Cameron's case the paradigm worked well. It almost always does.

Last week, Hampshire College emulated the worst decisions and instincts of those UMass administrators when it censored the Afrofunk band Shokazoba by unilaterally revoking the band's contract to perform. The American Association of University Professors' Guidelines, to which Hampshire pledges fidelity, state that in the event of controversy a college's invitation to a speaker or performer may be revoked only upon clear proof of an imminent and unavoidable threat to public safety. At Hampshire no one made any threat at all. So, you might ask, why was the band banned?

The Column

At a Hampshire College faculty meeting twenty years ago, a professor introduced a motion to affirm "the right of all members of the college community to the free expression of views in speech or in art without censorship." The motion stated that noncriminal expression should be protected on Hampshire's campus "without regard to the positions or perspectives embodied in that speech or art."

At a liberal arts institution, and especially at left-leaning, experimental, no grades, self-directed learning Hampshire College in Amherst, Massachusetts, you might well think that the faculty would unanimously support such a statement. But you'd be wrong. Dead wrong.

Some faculty vociferously objected because the endorsement of free speech, they said, took account of only one side of the argument and was reactionary. One professor dismissed the importance of free expression because "the First Amendment was written by a rich, white, male slave owner." After the faculty, by a small margin, defeated the motion, the college president cautioned against allowing the outside world to learn about that vote. The meeting, however, eventually was revealed in *The Shadow University: The Betrayal Of Liberty On America's Campuses*, co-authored by attorney Harvey Silverglate.

Now, twenty years after that faculty meeting, Hampshire College once again has sacrificed free expression on the altar of political correctness and homogeneity. On October 7, the college hired the Afrofunk band Shokazoba to play at a Halloween party. Two days before the show, some Hampshire students posted remarks on the Facebook event wall, asserting that it was inappropriate to hire what was mistakenly described as an "all-white afro-beat band"—notwithstanding that Shokazoba has performed since 2005 at, among other venues, black clubs in Harlem and that the band's lead singer is African-American. When the lead singer posted to try to clear the air, she was accused of not being black enough.

A Hampshire dean explained to members of the band, who had sought a meeting with her, that the band deserved to be cancelled because of their inflammatory remarks on the Facebook event wall. When band members asked the dean to point to any such remark, she couldn't because they had made none. (Apparently some person, not a Hampshire student, had posted racist remarks that had been removed. Hampshire College itself administered the Facebook page.) The final band member to arrive on campus to attend that meeting never made it to the dean's office. He was met by campus police who ordered him to leave immediately or face arrest.

Faculty, students, and administrators at Hampshire College have proffered various justifications for the censorship. The most repeated explanation has been that the band made a statement on Facebook that allegedly furthered a "post-racial and color-blind" ideology, which is viewed by Hampshire administrators as "unacceptable." Hold on to your seats. Here's the offending passage:

> Do we really still view the world biopically as black vs. white? Are we not, in actuality, all different shades of brown? Has it not become abundantly clear that we are a world community that needs to support

each other in art and love—not in derisiveness (sic)? We play afro beat inspired music with love, and respect. We would create our art with historical and cultural appreciation, and with an intention of bringing people together regardless of individual socio-economic background or ethnocentric origin.

These sentiments apparently are so antithetical to the official dogma that writing these words, expressing these thoughts, compelled the college to censor the band that has a member who expressed them.

To be sure, the college puts it differently. Hampshire administrators pronounced that a predominately white band that plays Afrofunk music should be condemned as guilty of "cultural appropriation." That cultural appropriation—or misappropriation—in the estimation of Hampshire's higher-ups justified the bludgeon of the censor and the revocation of Shokazoba's contract to play—not even at a celebration of African heritage, mind you—but at a Halloween party!

Where does that line of thinking lead us and where does it end? Is it all right for people of diverse backgrounds and integrated music groups to play blues, rock 'n 'roll, or jazz at Hampshire College? Are Eminem, Sly & The Family Stone, Booker T. & the M.G.'s, and Paul Simon now prohibited on campus?

By e-mail, the students, faculty, and administrators who succeeded in having Hampshire cancel Shokazoba joyously celebrated their success. That celebration of the censors, I believe, demonstrates a dearth of understanding of how easily today's censors can become tomorrow's censored. Those self-congratulatory communications fail to reflect even an inkling of understanding how much freedom their supposed victory has cost, of how sad an occasion this actually has been.

November 2013

AMERICA GOING TO POT

"Marijuana Legalized In Massachusetts." Expect that headline on Wednesday, November 9, 2016.

For years, public opinion polls across the United States have demonstrated widespread support to end marijuana prohibition. Unfortunately, politicians still paranoid of the moniker "soft on crime" or "soft on drugs" have waffled on this issue and waited for the people to lead.

And the people have. In 2008, Massachusetts citizens voted by a thirty percent margin, 65 to 35, to decriminalize possession of a small amount for personal use, replacing a criminal sanction with a rarely enforced 100 dollar civil penalty. Four years later, in 2012, Massachusetts joined eighteen other states when voters approved medical marijuana by a similar landslide margin, 63 to 37 percent.

Something else important happened in 2012 in the fight for sane marijuana policies. The states of Colorado and Washington flat-out legalized marijuana for personal use, creating a system of regulation and taxation. Some months later, Attorney General Eric Holder announced that the federal Department of Justice would not bust producers, sellers, and consumers of marijuana who conformed to their state's marijuana laws—notwithstanding that cannabis remains illegal under federal statutes.

On Tuesday, November 8, 2016, citizens in Massachusetts, as well as in a number of other states, can expect to see the question of legalization on the ballot.

The day-after-the-election newspapers undoubtedly will quote some police official or the president of the Massachusetts Family Institute as "vehemently opposing" legalization and predicting "dire results." Fortunately, the story also will include the view of law enforcement officials who believe that the marijuana prohibition has been ineffective, unnecessary, and unfair—a gargantuan waste of time and money that detracts from the police doing what they are supposed to do—fight actual crime.

LEAP (Law Enforcement Against Prohibition) will praise the vote as making Massachusetts safer by eliminating gangs and guns and laced pot—not to mention the stigma of arrest—from the calculus of marijuana use. The newspaper will go on to note that the sale of marijuana will be restricted to adults; that legalization, studies show, does not increase use of marijuana by young people; and that criminal sanctions will remain in place for unauthorized sale or distribution and for driving under the influence.

The story undoubtedly will credit Bay State Repeal with having put different versions of the ballot initiative on the 2014 ballot as nonbinding public policy questions and using those results to craft the precise language for the 2016 ballot proposal. The newspaper will also note that Bay State Repeal secured the necessary number of signatures for the initiative to appear on the 2016 ballot and then helped organize the successful grassroots campaign.

Between now and November 2016 one of the biggest fights—curiously—may occur between two groups that both favor legalization. One group, composed primarily of licensed medical marijuana growers (who likely will be grandfathered as the licensed marijuana suppliers) may oppose a person's right to home-grow a couple of plants for his or her own use. After all, we're talking lost market share and missed tax revenue. But the more rational position is that if people can cultivate their own tomatoes and grapes and make homebrew, they should be allowed to grow marijuana for their own use as well. Can we agree that home gardeners and commercial tomato growers coexist quite nicely and that we don't need local law enforcement surveillance drones peering through our bedroom windows to determine if someone is growing a pot plant?

The *Daily Hampshire Gazette* reporter who will attend the legalization victory party will quote one supporter as saying, "People will look back and wonder how it could have taken over eighty years to get from repeal of alcohol prohibition to the repeal of marijuana prohibition." Another supporter standing nearby will interject, "Because marijuana was viewed as a drug that blacks used, and criminal drug laws allowed the United States to imprison people of color and, of course, some white people were caught up in that dragnet as well."

That explanation is unassailable. Campaign slogans from the late 1960s and early 1970s drove a war on crime and drugs that transmogrified into a horrible, senseless, and expensive experiment in mass incarceration. As Attorney General Holder has pointed out, the United States, with only five percent of the world's population, now incarcerates almost twenty-five percent of the world's prisoners.

The final paragraph of the newspaper's story may include a human-interest note—about a sixty-something-year-old civil liberties lawyer at that victory party sitting alone, nursing a beer, looking pensive. When asked, "Why the long face?" the attorney will muse, "I can't help thinking about the millions and millions, the tens of millions, of people and families whose lives have been destroyed by these stupid drug laws."

When pressed to admit that the vote made him happy, his face will brighten, and he will say, "You bet. I've lived through many decades when I never dreamed I'd live to see this day."

December 2013

WHAT MIGHT HAVE BEEN

On a muggy morning in early August, my daughter Leah and I were standing on the balcony outside room 306 of the Lorraine Motel in Memphis, Tennessee—the place where Martin Luther King, Jr. was standing when he was murdered on April 14, 1968.

We already had looked through the plateglass window into the room, preserved as it had been that day—the small TV with a rabbit ears antenna and a clock radio with a face and hands, coffee cups on saucers on a tray. Room 306 of the Lorraine Motel is part of the National Civil Rights Museum.

In front of us, across the carport, behind the main part of the museum, we had an unobstructed view of the former Bessie Brewer's Rooming House and the bathroom window from which James Earl Ray shot Dr. King. Before we went up the stairs to the balcony of the Lorraine, we had walked through the rooming house and stood at that window and stared at that balcony and Dr. King's room. The former rooming house, too, is part of the museum.

One exhibit reviews the facts of Dr. King's assassination. It points out that Ray, after escaping from prison and before murdering Dr. King, had lived well and purchased cars even though he didn't have a job. Ray also secured sophisticated false identifications and, after the assassination, fled to Canada and England before he was apprehended.

The official government story says that James Earl Ray learned that Dr. King was staying at the Lorraine Motel from the *Commercial Appeal* newspaper that morning. The exhibit chillingly points out the evidence that Ray, under an alias, had rented a room at the Lorraine Motel two days earlier. The exhibit also notes that the FBI had Dr. King under twenty-four hour surveillance at that time, and after Ray shot King, the local police didn't notify law enforcement in the adjacent states of Ray's escape from Memphis.

Ray accepted a plea bargain of ninety-nine years in Tennessee's Brushy Mountain State Penitentiary in exchange for prosecutors dropping their request for the death penalty. We'll never know what a trial would have revealed, and the prosecution failed to demand a full accounting from Ray as part of the plea deal. Conspiracy theories have little allure for me, but it defies logic that Ray stalked and murdered King and then escaped all on his own.

Dr. King had come to Memphis in April 1968 to support the sanitation workers, on strike for a living wage and improvements in their deplorable and unsafe working conditions. He was staying at the Lorraine Motel because the downtown hotels were reserved for whites only.

While standing on the balcony of the Lorraine on a date close to the fiftieth anniversary of the march on Washington and the "I have a dream" speech and forty-five years after he was murdered, I struggled to fathom a fact I thought I knew well—that one moment Dr. Martin Luther King, the embodiment of hope for equality and economic justice at home and for peace in Vietnam, was standing right here—on this exact spot—and the next moment, he was dead.

Leah, who is twenty-seven, and I had stopped in Memphis as we were driving cross-country in her car that was filled with boxes and duffel bags and furniture. She was moving from San Francisco to Brooklyn.

Driving east on Route 40 out of Memphis on our way to Nashville, I found it nearly impossible to try to convey to Leah how insane the world felt at the time of Dr. King's assassination and—less than two months later—Bobby Kennedy's. Death and destruction felt omnipresent. In my lifetime, President Kennedy and Malcolm X also had been assassinated, and civil rights workers Andrew Goodman, Michael Schwerner, and James Chaney ("two Jews and a nigger," as some referred to them) had been murdered as well; and every day more and more kids were being shipped home from Vietnam in body bags.

As we drove, Leah and I speculated about what America would be today if Dr. King had not been murdered. Would we be closer to his dream? Would America have needlessly imprisoned millions of black men, victims of what white politicians call a war on crime and what civil rights advocate Michelle Alexander calls The New Jim Crow? Could his leadership have prevented the wars in Iraq and Afghanistan? With King as our moral watchman, would America have waged and won the war on poverty instead?

As Leah and I sat quietly for some moments listening to the sound of the tires on the highway, the words of John Greenleaf Whittier, the nineteenth-century poet and abolitionist, kept running through my mind: "For of all sad words of tongue or pen / the saddest are these: 'It might have been!'"

September 2013

Many Thanks

To my daughters Jo and Leah—for your love, your editorial suggestions on this manuscript, and for not freaking out too much when your father wrote about you in our local newspaper when you were teenagers;

To my clients whose stories are here—your courage and humanity and fights for dignity have breathed life into the constitutional promises of equality and freedom;

To my colleagues at the national ACLU and the ACLU of Massachu-setts—your work inspires me; your skill astounds me; as for the cases we have litigated and won together, I cannot give you credit or thanks enough;

To my readers Rita Bleiman, Cathi Hanauer, Elli Meeropol, Robby Meeropol, Rob Okun, Josh Wolk, and Jean Zimmer—for making this book better;

To Bryan Stevenson—for your inspiring commitment to fighting the death penalty and for reviewing some of the writing here on capital pun-ishment;

To Ray Levasseur—for your courage in surviving America's penal sys-tem and for commenting on "Marionizing Massachusetts";

To Kim Beaudry—for your skill, patience and persistence in typing a gazillion (give or take a few million) drafts, to Jone Messmer for her typ-ing help as well;

To Steve Strimer—for creating Levellers Press and having faith in this project;

To friends who appear in these pages, Buz Eisenberg, Elizabeth Fink, Diane Garey, David Hoose, Dusty Houser, Cora Kaplan, the late Anna Kirwan, Randy Kehler, Robby Meeropol, Pat Schneider, Wendy Sibbison and Barry Werth—for your commitment to social justice, your knowl-edge and insights, the beauty of the art and words that you have brought into the world, and your importance in my life;

To the editors at The *Daily Hampshire Gazette* and *Hampshire Life* magazine who have taken such good care of my writing—particularly Jim Foudy for asking me to write for the paper in the first place; Suzanne Wilson for showing me what a good editor does; and Larry Parnass for inviting me back;

To Dale, my best reader, Dale—most of all to Dale—without you this book would have never been. Whatever success I may have had in this life I owe to your love;

Finally and posthumously, to my mom and dad—I think about you every day. I carry memories of you close to my heart. I so wish you were here to read this book.